Social Issues in Literature

Race in the Poetry of Langston Hughes

Other Books in the Social Issues in Literature Series:

Class Conflict in Charles Dickens's *A Tale of Two Cities*

Coming of Age in Sue Monk Kidd's *The Secret Life of Bees*

The Environment in Rachel Carson's *Silent Spring*

Family Dysfunction in Tennessee Williams's *The Glass Menagerie*

Family Dysfunction in William Faulkner's *As I Lay Dying*

The Food Industry in Eric Schlosser's *Fast Food Nation*

Poverty in John Steinbeck's *The Pearl*

Race in John Howard Griffin's *Black Like Me*

Race in William Shakespeare's *Othello*

Sexuality in William Shakespeare's *A Midsummer Night's Dream*

War in Erich Maria Remarque's *All Quiet on the Western Front*

Wildness in Jack London's *The Call of the Wild*

Social Issues in Literature

Race in the Poetry of Langston Hughes

Claudia Durst Johnson, Book Editor

GREENHAVEN PRESS
A part of Gale, Cengage Learning

Detroit • New York • San Francisco • New Haven, Conn • Waterville, Maine • London

Elizabeth Des Chenes, *Director, Content Strategy*
Cynthia Sanner, *Publisher*
Douglas Dentino, *Manager, New Product*

© 2014 Greenhaven Press, a part of Gale, Cengage Learning

Gale and Greenhaven Press are registered trademarks used herein under license.

For more information, contact:
Greenhaven Press
27500 Drake Rd.
Farmington Hills, MI 48331-3535
Or you can visit our Internet site at gale.cengage.com

ALL RIGHTS RESERVED.
No part of this work covered by the copyright herein may be reproduced, transmitted, stored, or used in any form or by any means graphic, electronic, or mechanical, including but not limited to photocopying, recording, scanning, digitizing, taping, Web distribution, information networks, or information storage and retrieval systems, except as permitted under Section 107 or 108 of the 1976 United States Copyright Act, without the prior written permission of the publisher.

For product information and technology assistance, contact us at

Gale Customer Support, 1-800-877-4253
For permission to use material from this text or product, submit all requests online at www.cengage.com/permissions

Further permissions questions can be emailed to permissionrequest@cengage.com

Articles in Greenhaven Press anthologies are often edited for length to meet page requirements. In addition, original titles of these works are changed to clearly present the main thesis and to explicitly indicate the author's opinion. Every effort is made to ensure that Greenhaven Press accurately reflects the original intent of the authors. Every effort has been made to trace the owners of copyrighted material.

Cover image © Corbis.

LIBRARY OF CONGRESS CATALOGING-IN-PUBLICATION DATA

Race in the poetry of Langston Hughes / Claudia Durst Johnson, book editor.
  pages cm. -- (Social issues in literature)
Includes bibliographical references and index.
ISBN 978-0-7377-6980-7 (hardcover)
ISBN 978-0-7377-6981-4 (pbk.)
 1. Hughes, Langston, 1902-1967--Criticism and interpretation. 2. Race relations in literature. I. Johnson, Claudia Durst, 1938- editor of compilation.
 PS3515.U274Z6977 2013
 818'.5209--dc23

2013004522

Printed in the USA
 2 3 4 5 6   30 29 28 27 26

Contents

Introduction   9
Chronology   13

Chapter 1: Background on Langston Hughes

1. The Life of an Artist and Activist   16
   R. Baxter Miller

   Hughes's poetry was influenced by his early childhood poverty and later by African American music, race relations in the South, and the evils of racism and fascism on an international scale.

2. Hughes's Abolitionist Ancestors and Boyhood Segregation   28
   Arnold Rampersad

   Hughes, the descendant of abolitionists, experienced racial discrimination himself in his school years in Kansas.

Chapter 2: Race in the Poetry of Langston Hughes

1. The Social Messages in the Poetry of Langston Hughes   38
   Onwuchekwa Jemie

   Through his poetry, Hughes identifies himself as a Negro poet with a social message. He highlights a lost Africa, the truth of lynching and Jim Crow laws, and hope in a different America made possible with radical politics.

2. Langston Hughes + Poetry = The Blues   49
   Yusef Komunyakaa

   The musical art form of the blues has had a significant influence on Hughes's poetry. His poetry creates tension and conflict through its beats and verticalness. It also reflects the everyday lives of African Americans.

3. Langston Hughes: The Writer, His Poetics
and the Artistic Process
Martha Cobb

55

Hughes's poetry is a melding of individual talent and the folklore of his race. His poems are told in the traditional language and voice of the African American.

4. Hughes's Contradictory Reactions
to the Christian Church
Mary Beth Culp

64

Christianity is integral to African American life in both positive and negative ways. It is the white religion that justifies oppression and the African American religion that identifies Christ's martyrdom with the subjugated.

5. The Parental Rejection of the Tragic Mulatto
Arthur P. Davis

73

Hughes's tragic mulatto theme, in which a white father rejects the son of an African American mother, is mirrored in Hughes's abandonment by his own father, a black man who hated his race.

6. Hughes Took Advantage of the Tension
Between Style and Theme
Raymond Smith

82

Hughes made the conscious choice to write about race, although his views betrayed ambivalence about his subject.

7. The Politics of Hughes's Lynching Poems
W. Jason Miller

91

The omission of certain lynching poems from Hughes's collections was a result of the repressive 1950s. Public acceptance finally came by placing the poems in historical context.

8. Rage, Repudiation, and Endurance: Langston
Hughes's Radical Writings
Christopher C. DeSantis

99

Racial injustice was perpetuated not only by whites but also by black leaders. Hughes's radicalism is shown in his deference to Marxism, an ideology he repudiated after the pact the Soviet Union made with Adolf Hitler.

Chapter 3: Contemporary Perspectives on Race

1. Laws in 2011 and 2012 Are Designed to Diminish Minority Votes 117
   Wendy R. Weiser and Lawrence Norden

   In 2011 many states began to make laws discouraging voter registration drives and Sunday voting, making it harder for African Americans to vote.

2. Defusing Implicit Bias 126
   Jonathan Feingold and Karen Lorang

   The Trayvon Martin case has reawakened discussion about the connection between guns and racial discrimination. At issue are inadequate police training and "stand your ground laws."

3. An Actor with a Sense of Responsibility to Human and Civil Rights 135
   Stuart Jeffries

   Danny Glover stands out as one of the few black celebrities consistently working for racial justice and education worldwide—as a college student in California, later in Haiti, and as a lecturer on race throughout the world.

4. Alabama Looks for Way to Pardon Scottsboro Boys 143
   Phillip Rawls

   For decades, the public has believed the Scottsboro defendants were innocent, but laws in Alabama still stand in the way of their receiving posthumous pardons.

For Further Discussion	147
For Further Reading	148
Bibliography	149
Index	154

Introduction

Langston Hughes is regarded as the most distinguished African American social poet the United States has produced. A complete collection of his poems was issued by Arnold Rampersad and David Roessel in 1994; a third edition of the two-volume biography of Hughes was printed in 2003; and a society and a journal—the Langston Hughes Society and the *Langston Hughes Review*, respectively—are devoted to the study of his work. His standing has remained strong because he never lost sight of his racial roots and never abandoned his social message.

African and African American folklore and music were the strongest influences on his poetry, shaping its form and cadence. He was introduced to spirituals and gospel music in his teens when a family friend took him with her to church. His poems "Prayer Meeting" and "Spirituals" illustrate this experience. His elderly relatives, including his grandmother, told him stories of family history such as that of his ancestors' association with abolitionists and John Brown, as can be seen in his poems "The Raid" about John Brown and "Aunt Sue's Stories."

Hughes was born and spent most of his youth in the Midwest, scarcely an area steeped in the black rural culture of the South or the urban black society developed by African Americans who had been migrating to the North since the end of the Civil War. It was not until his teens that Hughes was introduced to the music that had the greatest influence on his poetry—the blues and jazz.

These musical forms were promoted by the African American artistic and cultural movement of the 1920s and 30s, in an African American area of New York City. It was called the

Harlem Renaissance. The artists and scholars who were part of this movement embraced, defined, and researched what it meant to be black in America.

The Harlem Renaissance, in all its glory, maintained a joyous, optimistic view of the emergence of "the New Negro," who had successfully challenged the stereotypes of the past. However, in the 1930s, the Harlem Renaissance would be confronted by a stark reality it could not ignore—the Great Depression. The starving homeless people sleeping in doorways and the unemployed armies of families living in shacks were in stark contrast to the euphoria of black progress. Hughes, in his first autobiography, confesses a turning point—when he realized that his artistic lifestyle was phony and cruel in light of the poverty, particularly among African Americans.

The subject matter of Hughes's poetry has to be considered against the historical issues that impacted him. The principal ones in this country were the racism that escalated in the 1920s and 30s, resulting in more and more lynchings, as whites competed with blacks for the few jobs available; the Scottsboro case that erupted in 1931 in which nine black men were wrongly accused of rape by two white women; the persistence of Jim Crow laws that legalized discrimination and segregation; the Red Scare of the 1950s, during which left-wing citizens were harassed and lost their jobs and reputations; and, finally, the civil rights movement of the 1950s and 60s.

Hughes was a prominent figure in all of this history. In 1927 and 1931 he visited the South, where he found a more repugnant racism than he had ever experienced firsthand. Some of his angriest poems are about the South's racial injustice, such as "Christ in Alabama," "Open Letter to the South," and "Goodbye Christ."

The Scottsboro trials that began in 1931—a year that Hughes spent in the South and West—became, in the artist's eyes, a paradigm for the South's racial injustice. During this year, he visited the defendants in prison with the hope of amusing them with funny poems. He became involved in the politics of their defense. In 1932 he published a play and four poems in one volume, titled *Scottsboro Limited*. One of the poems was dedicated to one of the defendants, "August 19th . . . A Poem for Clarence Norris."

In the 1930s many Americans were turning to radical politics for answers to their misery. Many argued that American Communists were the only people working effectively for the poor. Having already read German philosopher Karl Marx and Russian Communist revolutionary Vladimir Lenin, Hughes visited the Soviet Union in 1932. This visit and his revolutionary writings, such as the poems "Chant for May Day" and "Lenin," made him the target of conservative public outrage. After World War II, Congress began formal investigations into anyone suspected of having leftist leanings. It was no surprise that Hughes was called before the Senate Permanent Subcommittee on Investigations in 1953. Having infuriated the right, now he infuriated the left, by calling his earlier radical works mistakes and testifying that he no longer believed that communism could be justified.

Yet he persevered to work for racial progress with the National Association for the Advancement of Colored People (NAACP) and to write poems about special racial problems besetting Americans. Some titles illustrative of this are "Ku Klux Klan," "Freedom's Plough," "Governor Fires Dean," and "Bible Belt."

The following viewpoints focus on the issue of race in the poetry of Langston Hughes. The first chapter contains entries about his life and the inspiration for his social commitment. Chapter two contains viewpoints that explore the relevance to race in his poetry—the black culture that shaped the form of his poetry and the social message poems that became his hallmark. The topics include Hughes's rejection of the traditional African American church, the plight of the biracial child, lynching, and a poet discouraged by ineffective leaders. Chapter three examines some racial issues in contemporary America, such as voting rights, the Trayvon Martin case, the current relevancy of the Scottsboro trials, hip-hop music, current black leaders, racial profiling, and discrimination in law enforcement and prisons.

Chronology

1902
Hughes is born in Joplin, Missouri. His father leaves the family and the United States.

1907–1920
Hughes lives in different places throughout the Midwest, graduating from high school in Cleveland, Ohio.

1921
Hughes enrolls at Columbia University, having already begun publishing poems.

1923–1924
Hughes travels to Africa and Europe.

1926
The Weary Blues, Hughes's first book of poems, is published, and he enters Lincoln University, from which he graduates in 1929.

1927
Hughes meets his patroness, who supports his work for three years, and he begins to publish fiction and plays.

1931
Hughes begins a trip to the South and participates in the defense of the Scottsboro defendants.

1932–1940
Hughes visits the Soviet Union and other countries abroad and distinguishes himself in a number of genres.

1939
Hughes writes the script for *Way Down South*, a movie.

1941
Hughes begins a column in the *Chicago Defender*.

1943
Jim Crow's Last Stand is published.

1950
Simple Speaks His Mind in published by Simon & Schuster.

1951
Montage of a Dream Deferred is published.

1952
A collection of short stories, *Laughing to Keep from Crying*, is published.

1953
Hughes appears before the Senate Permanent Subcommittee on Investigations.

1961
Ask Your Mama: 12 Moods for Jazz is published.

1967
Hughes dies on May 22.

Social Issues in Literature

CHAPTER 1

Background on Langston Hughes

The Life of an Artist and Activist

R. Baxter Miller

R. Baxter Miller, professor of English at the University of Georgia, is author or editor of ten books, including On the Ruins of Modernity.

Langston Hughes's early life was poverty stricken and unstable. His father abandoned the family and moved to Mexico, where Hughes had tense, unpleasant visits with him. He began writing poetry when he was in his teens and at nineteen began both domestic and overseas travel—trips that proved to educate Hughes in the power of racism and fascism throughout the world. Some of his earliest foreign trips were to Africa, where he found his spiritual roots. A turning point in his life was a 1931 trip to a part of the world he had never seen—the American South. There he encountered, for the first time, the extreme segregation and discrimination in what had been the heart of slavery. This experience, more than any other, focused his poetry on social issues. His trips to Russia familiarized him with socialism and made him a target of federal investigations in the 1950s and 60s.

Few writers become household names, yet such is the case of Langston Hughes, who was perhaps the most significant black American writer in the twentieth century. His poems, novels, short stories, dramas, translations, and anthologies of the works of others span the period from the early days of the Harlem Renaissance in the 1920s to the black arts movement in the late 1960s. His early work was influenced by his contact with contemporary creative figures such as Countee Cullen,

---

R. Baxter Miller, "(James) Langston Hughes," *Afro-American Writers from the Harlem Renaissance to 1940*, ed. Trudier Harris-Lopez and Thadious M. Davis, vol. 51, 1987, pp. 1–18. From Trudier Harris/Thadious Davis, Afro-American Writers from the Harlem Renaissance to 1940, 0E. © 1986 Cengage Learning. Reproduced by permission.

Aaron Douglas, and Josephine Baker. In his late twenties and early thirties, he helped to inspire writers Margaret Walker and Gwendolyn Brooks. Later he encouraged writers of a third generation, including Ted Joans, Alice Walker, and Mari Evans.

Between 1921 and 1967 Hughes became both famous and loved. Even before he had helped young blacks gain entry to the major periodicals and presses of the day, his innovations in literary blues and jazz were acclaimed. As he worked to free American literature from the plantation tradition, he introduced new forms that reflected confidence and racial pride. He displayed social awareness in his fictional characters and technical mastery in his works.

The Effect of Childhood Poverty

James Mercer Langston Hughes was born to Carrie Langston Hughes and James Nathaniel Hughes on 1 February 1902 in Joplin, Missouri. Carrie's father, Charles Howard Langston, moved to Kansas in search of greater racial and financial freedom. His penchant for the literary and his desire to transcend the farm and the grocery store in Lawrence, Kansas, were passed on to Hughes. Charles's brother, John Mercer Langston, the poet's great-uncle, contributed to the family's literary efforts by penning an autobiography, *From the Virginia Plantation to the National Capital* (1894). The financially secure John Mercer Langston willed to his descendants a big house as well as stocks and bonds.

Hughes's mother, Carrie Langston, had briefly attended college, and she demonstrated a dramatic imagination through writing poetry and delivering monologues in costume. James Nathaniel Hughes, the poet's father, studied law by correspondence course, but when he was denied permission by the all-white examining board to take the Oklahoma Territory bar examination, he moved to Joplin with his wife in 1899. There, after four years of marriage and the death of his first child (in

1900), angered by unremitting poverty and faced with supporting an eighteen-month-old child, James Hughes left the United States in October 1903 for Mexico, where he eventually prospered and thus was able to contribute to the support of his son. Carrie Hughes refused to accompany him, and, unable to get even menial jobs in Joplin, she moved constantly from city to city looking for work, occasionally taking the young Langston with her. For most of the next nine years, however, the poet lived in Lawrence with his maternal grandmother, Mary Leary Langston, although he visited his mother briefly in Topeka, stayed with her in Colorado, and traveled with her to Mexico in 1908 to see his father.

As a youngster, Hughes was acutely aware of the luxury in which his cousins lived in Washington in contrast to the poverty in which he and his grandmother lived, but she never wrote to them for help. He learned early that bills do not always get paid but that resourcefulness was essential to survival. Unlike most other black women in Lawrence, Kansas, his grandmother did not earn money by domestic service. She rented rooms to college students from the University of Kansas, and sometimes she would even live with a friend and rent out her entire house for ten or twelve dollars a month....

Hughes's grandmother influenced his life and imagination deeply. She was a gentle and proud woman of Indian and black blood. He remembered that she once took him to Osawatomie. There, she shared the platform as an honored guest of Teddy [Theodore] Roosevelt because she was the last surviving widow of the 1859 John Brown raid. Following her death in April 1915, Hughes lived briefly with his mother who had by then (possibly in the previous year) married Homer Clark. When Clark left town to seek a job elsewhere, Carrie Hughes left Langston with his grandmother's friend Auntie Reed and her husband, who owned a house a block from the river and near the railroad station....

In the seventh grade, Hughes secured his first regular job—cleaning the lobby and toilets in an old hotel near school. . . .

The Influence of the Blues on Hughes's Early Poetry

During the winter of 1923 Hughes wrote the poem that would give the title to his first volume of poetry. "The Weary Blues," about a piano player in Harlem, captures the flavor of the night life, people, and folk forms that would become characteristic of the experimental writing of the renaissance. The piano player uses his instrument to create the "call and response" pattern essential to the blues. He is alone and lonely: "Ain't got nobody in all this world, / Ain't got nobody but ma self. / I's gwine to quit ma frownin' / And put ma troubles on the shelf," but his piano "talks" back to him. Through the process of playing the piano and singing about his troubles, the man is able to exorcise his feelings and arrive at a state of peace:

>And far into the night he crooned that tune.
>
>The stars went out and so did the moon.
>
>The singer stopped playing and went to bed
>
>While the Weary Blues echoed through his head.
>
>He slept like a rock or a man that's dead.

In structure and subject matter the poem varies from traditional forms. Although there are rhymes and onomatopoeic effects ("Thump, thump, thump, went his foot on the floor"), there are also unusual lines, such as

>Sweet Blues!
>
>Coming from a black man's soul.
>
>O Blues!

Langston Hughes was a prolific poet and author, from the 1920s through the 1960s, known for his portrayals of black life in America. © Corbis.

Such lines serve to move the poem beyond its traditional components and to locate the ethos in Afro-American culture. A frequently anthologized poem, "The Weary Blues" treats blues as theme and structure and was a fitting choice as the title of a volume designed to focus on the masses of black people rather than the elite....

Background on Langston Hughes

After a brief visit to Lincoln, Illinois, in February 1926, Hughes enrolled at Lincoln University in Pennsylvania. When classes were over for the summer, he moved to New York....

In New York that summer Hughes wrote and rewrote the poem, "Mulatto," which would appear in *Saturday Review of Literature* and in the collection *Fine Clothes to the Jew* (1927). When he read the poem one evening at James Weldon Johnson's, Clarence Darrow called it the most moving poem he had heard. While Hughes himself said the verse was about "white fathers and Negro mothers in the South," the craft transcends the autobiographical paraphrase. Through the view of one son, a victim of miscegenation, the speaker judges the father's contemptuous indifference and illustrates the callousness of white America in particular and humanity in general. Finally, he shows the hatred of the legitimate son for the bastard speaker, for the former signifies the inner collapse of the human family through racism.

"Mulatto" reinforces the techniques used in the ballad "Cross," published earlier but also collected in *Fine Clothes to the Jew*. In the poems Hughes enlarged the basic inequality among blacks into social and symbolic meaning, the "problem of mixed blood ... one parent in the pale of the black ghetto and the other able to take advantage of all the opportunities of American democracy." He also emphasized the peculiar plight of the mulatto. "Cross" proclaims:

My old man died in a fine big house.

My ma died in a shack.

I wonder where I'm gonna die,

Being neither white nor black? ...

The Shock of the South

[Years later,] Hughes received a grant for $1,000 from the Rosenwald Fund to tour black colleges in the South. He purchased a Ford and then, having no license, he struck a deal with Lucas Radcliffe, a fellow alumnus of Lincoln. Radcliffe would drive and manage accounts while he would read poetry. Both men would share the profits.

The trip, starting in the fall of 1931, deepened Hughes's commitments to racial justice and literary expression. When the nine Scottsboro boys were accused unjustly of raping two white prostitutes, he observed unhappily that black colleges were silent. "Christ in Alabama," a poem comparing the silence of the black colleges to that of the bystanders at the Crucifixion, caused a sensation in Chapel Hill, North Carolina, where playwright Paul Green and sociologist Guy B. Johnson had invited Hughes to read in November. About a week before the scheduled arrival, Hughes received a note from a white student, Anthony Buttita, who invited him to share a room. Buttita and his roommate, Milton Abernethy, had printed two of Hughes's publications, "Christ in Alabama" and an article, in *Contempo*, an unofficial student magazine. The poem had included lines such as:

Christ is a Nigger

Beaten and black—

O, bare your back.

. . . .

Most holy bastard

Of the bleeding mouth:

Nigger Christ

On the cross of the South.

The subsequent appearance by Hughes nearly caused a riot, but his rescue from the angry crowd that attended the reading did not deter his challenge to racial segregation. He ate with the editors in a Southern restaurant and thereby helped to set a new tone for race relations in Chapel Hill. . . .

The Influence of Russian Ideology

The 1932 trip, which ended in San Francisco (at the home of Noel Sullivan, who would later be helpful to Hughes) after stops in Arkansas and other places, encouraged the literary relationships which shaped Hughes's imaginative life and made him speculate on both the nature and the obligation of art. This heightened awareness framed his journey to Russia that year as part of a film company. When Hughes met Arthur Koestler, the Hungarian-born British writer in Ashkhabad, the two explored Soviet Asia together. Koestler provided the opportunity for Hughes to reflect on emotion and creativity: "There are many emotional hypochondriacs on earth, unhappy when not happy, sad when not expounding on their sadness. Yet I have always been drawn to such personalities because I often feel sad inside myself, too, though not inclined to show it. Koestler wore his sadness on his sleeve." Schooled in Western individualism, Hughes defended the artist's autonomy against the political directives of bureaucrats. Koestler retorted that the simultaneous expression of politics and individuality were difficult, especially when politicians lacked appreciation for creativity. At certain moments, Koestler argued, social aims transcended personal desires, though the Russian writer had begun to see Stalinist repression [under dictator Joseph Stalin] and to turn against communism. Grateful for the discussions with Koestler, Hughes probably thought his own ideas unchanged, but the encounter had renewed his leftist inclinations....

In Russia Hughes had learned well the relationship between writing and mythmaking. The representative of a leading American newspaper had intentionally printed a story in New York that the film company with which Hughes was traveling was stranded and starving in Moscow. When the filmmakers showed the reporter the clippings, he merely grinned. But Hughes, to provide a clearer picture, praised the many positive changes which Americans ignored in revolutionized

Russia, particularly the open housing and reduced persecution of Jews. Yet Hughes turned away from Russia eventually because he refused to live without jazz, which the Communists banned, for they limited artistic freedom generally.

Hughes Gets More Involved Politically

Determined to confront worldwide fascism and racism, Hughes returned to San Francisco by way of the Orient in 1933. His trip home demonstrates his headstrong personality. Though Westerners in Shanghai had warned him that the watermelons were tainted and potentially fatal there, he ate well, enjoyed the fruit, and lived to write the story. Warned to avoid the Chinese districts, he visited those areas and found the danger illusory. In Tokyo the police interrogated, detained, and finally expelled him. In the Japanese press's inflated stories of Korean crimes, he read the pattern of racism so familiar in the states. Aware that victims become victimizers in turn, he understood the Japanese debasement of the Chinese, and, on the way back to the United States, he warned that Japan was a fascist country.

Between 1933 and 1934 Hughes retired temporarily from world politics. In Carmel, at Sullivan's home "Ennesfree," he completed a series of short stories, which were later included in *The Ways of White Folks*. He also wrote articles, including one on the liberation of women from the harems of Soviet Asia. Grateful to Noel Sullivan for the time to write, Hughes worked from ten to twelve hours a day, producing at least one story or article every week and earning more money than he ever had. He sent most of his earnings to his mother, who was ill at the time. Having broken with his father in 1922, Hughes learned, too late to attend the funeral, that his father had died in Mexico on 22 October 1934....

Hughes's Reputation Grows

Hughes's work continued to earn public recognition from 1938 to 1967, the year of his death. The poems in *A New Song*

(1938) are politically sensitive and direct, yet replete with social irony and personal determination. "Let America Be America Again" shows the loss of an ideal, yet invokes the reappearance of it. Through the images of eye sores, the satirical poem, "Justice," emphasizes social blindness. . . .

When *Shakespeare in Harlem* had been published, Hughes returned to New York. For a while he shared a three-room apartment with . . . two old family friends, and he wrote verses and slogans to help sell U.S. Defense Bonds. In a weekly column for the *Chicago Defender*, a black newspaper, he began to publish the tales of Jesse B. Semple—later called Jesse B. Simple—a folk philosopher who would capture the hearts of thousands of readers. In 1946 he won a medal and prize of $1,000 from the American Academy of Arts and Letters. In the early months of 1947 he served as visiting professor of creative writing at Atlanta University. For a few weeks in 1949 he was poet in residence at the Laboratory School of the University of Chicago. . . .

However modern he was, Langston Hughes would never abandon black folk life for Western imagism. In *Montage of a Dream Deferred* (1951), his first book-length poem, dramatic and colloquial effects challenged his lyricism. Numerous projects in the writing of history and short fiction, such as *The First Book of Negroes* (1952) and *Simple Takes a Wife* (1953), drained his poetic energies. His style became more sophisticated. Through monologue and free verse, he stressed dramatic situations and mastered the apostrophe. In blending content with form, he fused narrative with sound effects. . . .

After testifying in 1953 before the Senate subcommittee chaired by Joseph McCarthy [who initiated investigations of alleged Communist sympathizers] investigating the purchase of books by subversive writers for American libraries abroad, Hughes received fewer offers to read poems over the next several years but enhanced the craft of his fiction. When *The Best of Simple* (1961) appeared he had developed a comic veneer and lightness which concealed complex symbolism artfully. Through urban dialect he had juxtaposed the seriousness of the Great Migration [referring to the movement of millions of blacks out of the American South to other parts of the country] in Simple's past with the humorous tone of the moment. Simple's folk imagination struck a balance with the polished reason of Boyd, his bar buddy. . . .

In 1960 Hughes visited Paris for the first time in twenty-two years, and he would from then on make many trips on cultural grants from the State Department—an irony indeed, since until 1959 he was on the "security index" of the FBI's [Federal Bureau of Investigation's] New York office. He would visit Africa a number of times, and revisit Europe. The year 1961 saw the publication of Hughes's crowning achievement. *Ask Your Mama* is as much Juvenalian as Horatian [referring to Roman poets and satirists Juvenal and Horace, respectively] in its satiric response to the rising anger of the 1960s. Fusing poetry with jazz, Hughes interweaves myth and history. He moves now into the child's mind and then into the man's; he reverses himself and begins afresh. Through fantasy, travesty, allusion, and irony, he depicts singers, actors, writers, politicians, and musicians. With a deepened imagination, he draws upon the rich themes of his entire career, such as humanism, free speech, transitoriness, and assimilation; nationalism, racism, integration, and poverty. He speculates about Pan-Africanism and personal integrity. Praising Hughes's commitment to universal freedom, Rudi Blesh called *Ask Your Mama* "a half angry and half derisive retort to the bigoted, smug, stupid, selfish, and blind." . . .

Following Hughes's death, critical commentary was respectful. Reviewing *The Panther & the Lash* (1967), Bill Katz praised the writer's commitment to diverge from both liberal and reactionary views of race. Lamine Diakhaté called Hughes a "pilgrim who affirmed the identity of man in the face of the absurd . . . showed the problems of blacks in a democratic society, restored the rhythmical language of Africa introduced by jazz in America, and demonstrated inextinguishable hope." François Dodat noted Hughes's humanistic faith. Most celebrators mention the writer's great generosity.

Hughes's Abolitionist Ancestors and Boyhood Segregation

Arnold Rampersad

Professor emeritus at Stanford University, Arnold Rampersad is the author of numerous books of biography and literary criticism; an editor; and a holder of the MacArthur Foundation fellowship.

Langston Hughes's ancestors hold noteworthy places in African American history and passed down to him an obligation to his race. One of his ancestors was a white planter who chose a black woman for his spouse. One of this couple's sons fought against slavery; another served in Congress. Another of Hughes's ancestors was killed fighting with John Brown at Harpers Ferry. Hughes, who lived much of his childhood moving from place to place in the Midwest, had his first personal experience with racism in the segregated school system of Topeka, Kansas. When his mother finally got him admitted to the white school closer to their home, he was cruelly berated by his teacher. In Lawrence, Kansas, he continued to be confronted by segregation in the schools, the YMCA, the Boy Scouts, and athletic teams. He was introduced to black culture as a teenager and was deeply influenced by the music of the church.

As successful as his life seemed to be by its end, with honors and awards inspired by more than forty books, and the adulation of thousands of readers, Hughes's favorite phonograph record over the years, spun in his bachelor suite late into the Harlem night, remained Billie Holiday's chilly moan-

---

Arnold Rampersad, *The Life of Langston Hughes Volume 1: 1902–1941: I, Too, Sing America*, 2002, pp. 4–4, 12–17, 22. Copyright © Oxford University Press. All rights reserved. Reproduced by permission.

ing of "God Bless the Child That's Got His Own." Eventually he had gotten his own, but at a stiff price. He had paid in years of nomadic loneliness and a furtive sexuality; he would die without ever having married, and without a known lover or a child. If by the end he was also famous and even beloved, Hughes knew that he had been cheated early of a richer emotional life. Parents could be so cruel! "My theory is," he wrote not long before he died, "children should be born without parents—if born they must be."

Hughes's Forebears Defined Him

Whatever Hughes's theory about parents, however, he was also born into a relationship with his family's past, into a relationship with history, so intimate as to be almost sensual. Much was expected by his ancestors. They demanded, from the moment his elders recognized the boy's unusual intelligence and began to talk to him about duty and the race, that he had a messianic obligation to the Afro-American people, and through them to America. Among these ghostly but commanding figures were a white Virginia planter, the poet's great-grandfather, who had defied the mores of the South to live with the black woman he loved and their children; two of their sons—one who risked almost everything in fighting against slavery and segregation, another who had also fought for freedom but lived to serve in the U.S. Congress and represent his country in Haiti; a black hero killed at Harpers Ferry in John Brown's band; and John Brown himself, an ancestor of Langston Hughes by virtue of the blood spilled there. For these men, their best spokesman in Hughes's youth would be his proud, tale-telling grandmother; from their demands, ironically aided by parental neglect, which made him anxious for love and a settled identity, would come much of the purpose of his life. . . .

Mostly he lived with his maternal grandmother, "a small woman, brown, slightly bent, with very long hair almost to her waist and only slightly gray in places. . . . Her face was very wrinkled like an Indian squaw's." Mary Sampson Patterson Leary Langston was almost seventy years old when Langston was born. He remembered her spending most of her time in an old-fashioned rocking chair; except to attend the weekly meeting of her lodge, Mary Langston generally stayed at home. At night she read a chapter of the Bible, combed out her long hair, rolled it under a white nightcap, and went to bed. "She never shouted or got happy, and at night when she knelt down and prayed, she prayed silently." But she also read to her grandson from Grimm's [German brothers'] fairy tales, or from the Bible and whatever magazines and newspapers she could afford. Or she held him in her lap and in a calm, clipped voice related tales of heroism, of slavery and freedom, and especially of brave men and women who had striven to aid the colored race. "Through my grandmother's stories always life moved, moved heroically toward an end," Hughes would recall. But of black folkways, so important later to her grandson, she said nothing. "She had been away from the South since her youth so she evidently did not remember any Negro folk-stories. At least, she never told me any.". . .

Hughes's First Experience with Segregation and Discrimination

His most memorable early encounter with segregation came in the late summer of 1908, when he was ready to start school. Carrie Hughes [his mother] tried to place him in the first grade class of the nearby Harrison Street School in Topeka, but was rebuffed and told to take him instead to the Washington School for colored children across the railroad tracks, a considerable distance away. Carrie argued with the principal that she worked every day, and that Langston was too small a child to go through the city streets alone. When the principal, Eli S. Foster, refused to admit him, she appealed directly to the school board, argued her case, and won. (Ironically, in

1954 another victory over the Topeka Board of Education, before the U.S. Supreme Court, would mark the official end of segregation in the United States.)

Victory came at a price: Hughes began school a doubly marked child, black and a troublemaker. His teacher seemed to some people gentle and kind, but from the first day she tried to break him. Seating everyone but Langston alphabetically, she installed the baffled child deep in a corner, at the end of the last row. She peppered him with unkind remarks even after it was clear that he was a superior student. One day she took licorice sticks away from a white boy. "You don't want to eat these," she said loudly for the class to hear; "they'll make you black like Langston. You don't want to be black, do you?" At midterm she graded him "excellent" in three of his five subjects, but still taunted him. Some of his schoolmates slapped, stoned, or snowballed him on his way home; to his defense came other children, white themselves, from his neighborhood. Nevertheless, Langston did not lose his liking for school. His clothes neatly pressed each night by his mother, already in love with compliments, he was a model student.

In mid-April 1909, before the end of his first school year, Carrie Hughes withdrew Langston from Harrison and returned him to Lawrence and his grandmother. Carrie herself was off to Colorado Springs, Colorado, where on a visit that summer the boy saw unforgettable mountains with great white pointed peaks rising above the clouds. At the end of the summer, however, he was back with his grandmother in Lawrence. By this time, Mary Langston was past seventy and seldom left her home. Once, she took him to Topeka to hear a speech by the greatest colored man in the world, Booker T. Washington, the head of Tuskegee Institute in Alabama. On another rare excursion, she and Langston went to Osawatomie, Kansas, on August 31, 1910, for the dedication of the John Brown Memorial Battlefield there. As the last surviving widow of the Harpers Ferry force, Mary Langston was given a seat of honor on the platform (as Hughes later remembered). With the spirit of John Brown at hand, former president Theodore Roosevelt delivered his almost radical, celebrated "New Nationalism" speech, in which he stressed the primacy of humanity over property rights, and called for a powerful central government to curb big business and to reform the courts. For Mary Langston, the event was the last, long-delayed honor of her life; for her grandson, only eight years old and largely unconscious of its meaning, it was an unacknowledged summing up of the radical heritage to which he belonged by birth, and a prophecy of his life to come.

When Mary Langston stayed at home and forbade her grandson to go out after school, one reason was her hatred of segregation. Because blacks were refused membership in the church of her choice, which was probably Presbyterian, she attended no church at all. Some segregation, however, was beyond her control. When Hughes entered the second grade of the Pinckney School in the late summer of 1909, he joined the other black children of the first three grades in one classroom supervised by a black schoolteacher. (Curiously, integration began in the fourth grade.) Nevertheless, he was fortunate in his teacher. Remembering Charles Langston as a "deep thinker," Mary J. Dillard was touched by his grandson. At seven years, Langston was "a dreamy little boy," but very good in class. Outside of the classroom, however, Langston and the other black children knew the harsher side of segregation. White children could swim freely at the YMCA and join the Boy Scouts; blacks could do neither. Colored boys could not take part in the grammar school track meets, play on the school teams, or form a team to play against whites. The Patee Theater on Massachusetts Street used to admit blacks; then one day, when Langston put down his coin, the woman in the box office pushed it back and pointed to a new sign: NO COLORED ADMITTED. "Your people can't come anymore," she told Langston. Until the Bowersock Opera House opened

Background on Langston Hughes

On October 16, 1859, John Brown led a group of abolitionist insurgents to Harpers Ferry, West Virginia, where they briefly seized the US arsenal. Although John Brown, the leader of the raid, was tried and hung, his actions generated sympathy for the abolitionist cause. © Corbis.

in January 1912, . . . he could only listen wistfully while his white friends talked of the latest exploits of Charlie Chaplin, Dustin Farnum, and Mary Pickford. . . .

A Late Introduction to Black Culture

Sometimes his grandmother rented a room in her home to black students at the university; at other times she moved out entirely in order to rent the whole house, and lived with friends. Her economies sometimes upset her grandson. "She kept me neatly and cleanly pressed, but she did not mind my wearing made over clothes . . . or even the shoes women would give her for herself and which were very embarrassing to a boy to have to wear. She would always say, 'It is not what you wear, it is what you *are* that counts.' But other children were inclined to make fun of what one wore."

Mary Langston's economizing led, however, to a friendship that would be of great importance to the man Langston would become. In 1909, 1913, and 1914, according to city directories,

Mary Langston lived not at her home but at 731 New York Street in Lawrence. Between 1909 and the day in 1915 he left town for good, Langston probably lived at least three times at 731 New York Street, the home of James W. Reed and his wife, Mary. Born a slave in Missouri, "Uncle" Reed was a ditch digger and pipe layer for the local Kennedy Plumbing Company. "Auntie" Reed, some fifteen years younger, was a longtime resident of Lawrence and a member of St. Luke's Church, where she ran the Sunday school....

"For me," Hughes would write, "there have never been any better people in the world. I loved them very much." Tiny but energetic and indomitable, Auntie Reed made only one demand of Langston—attendance at her Sunday school. He grumbled a little, and dated his dislike of church from one translucent spring morning when he was forced to stay indoors to memorize verses from the Bible. Through Mary Reed, however, a fresh window opened on the black race and the world, one shut tight at his grandmother's house. Mary Reed was a Methodist Episcopal, but she carried no grudge against the black Baptists over on Warren Street. In fact, the focal point of Sunday, apart from church service and the Sunday school, became the forum of the Warren Street Baptist Church. There, university students and talented townsfolk gathered to sing and play classical music, recite poetry, read original essays and other compositions, and discuss the affairs of the day, especially as they affected the race....

On a visit to Kansas City he became aware of yet another aspect of black culture on which he would draw later as an artist and an individual. At an open air theatre on Independence Avenue, from an orchestra of blind musicians, Hughes first heard the blues. The music seemed to cry, but the words somehow laughed. The effect on him was one of piercing sadness, as if his deepest loneliness had been harmonized. He would remember the refrain of one song he heard, and employ it brilliantly at a crucial point in his career as a poet:

I got de Weary Blues

And I can't be satisfied.

Got de Weary Blues

And can't be satisfied—I

ain't happy no mo'

And I wish that I had died . . .

Between the church and the blues singers, and in spite of his youth and his cloistered life with Mary Langston, the world of black feeling and art opened before Langston. He neither felt religion nor could sing the blues, and yet both the religious drama and the secular music soothed and diverted him from his sense of solitude. They also alerted him to a power and a privacy of language residing in the despised race to which he belonged; approaching the church and the blues as an outsider, because of his grandmother's own forbidding distance, Langston only respected them the more. . . .

He Starts to Fill His Ancestors' Shoes at an Early Age

Entering the seventh grade at the Central School in 1914, Langston passed into the care of a white teacher who decided to institute segregated seating in her class. She either compelled or induced all the black children to move to a separate row. Langston moved with the rest, but with mounting anger. His teacher had not reckoned on someone of Langston's background—the legacy of Harpers Ferry, his grandfather's fierce speeches, his grandmother's pride. Printing cards that said JIM CROW ROW, Langston defiantly propped one on each black child's desk. When she bore down on him, he flew into the school yard screaming that his teacher had a Jim Crow row, she had a Jim Crow row. An administrator tried to restrain him, but Langston fought off the man. He was expelled. Led by a black doctor, a delegation of parents visited the school to complain about the teacher's actions; Carrie Hughes also arrived to plead her son's case. Finally he was reinstated. But the idea of Jim Crow seating was dropped....

The Need for Approval of His Race

At thirteen, Hughes probably already viewed the black world both as an insider and, far more importantly, an outsider. The view from outside did not lead to clinical objectivity, much less alienation. Once outside, every intimate force in Hughes would drive him back toward seeking the love and approval of the race, which would become the grand obsession of his life. Already he had begun to identify not his family but the poorest and most despised blacks as the object of his ultimate desire to please. He would *need* the race, and would need to appease the race, to an extent felt by few other blacks, and by no other important black writer. This psychological craving was a quality far more rare than race pride or a merely defensive antagonism against whites; it originated in an equally rare combination of a sense of racial destiny with a keen knowledge of childhood hurt.

Social Issues in Literature

CHAPTER 2

Race in the Poetry of Langston Hughes

The Social Messages in the Poetry of Langston Hughes

Onwuchekwa Jemie

Onwuchekwa Jemie, a Nigerian scholar, received his PhD from Harvard University and taught in American universities before returning to Nigeria, where he edits Nigeria Business Day. *His canonic book is* Toward the Decolonization of African Literature.

The tradition of African American writing, from slave narratives to that of 1960s radicals, has been to draw a precise picture of race in a white-dominated civilization. Langston Hughes is part of that tradition. His subjects are groups and individuals irreparably damaged by a racist society. He writes of African Americans as a despised race of people who have been torn from their African beginnings. Wrenched from their African paradise, they have become imprisoned in an unnatural world of skyscrapers and greed. To survive, they wear a comical, stereotypical mask to hide their rage at their condition. Their music conveys hope that has no basis in reality. Fulfillment is always in the distant future—a dream, but a dream deferred. Hughes reveals a link between victims of lynching and the crucified Jesus. The only hope for a misplaced, persecuted race will come through social revolution.

Amiri Baraka (LeRoi Jones) once defined the black writer's function as follows:

> The Black Artist's role in America is to aid in the destruction of America as he knows it. His role is to report and reflect so precisely the nature of the society, and of himself in

---

Onwuchekwa Jemie, "Or Does It Explode?," *Langston Hughes: An Introduction to the Poetry*, 1976, pp. 97–103, 108, 112–113, 120. Copyright © 1976 by Onwuchekwa Jemie. All rights reserved. Reproduced by permission.

that society, that other men will be moved by the exactness of his rendering and, if they are black men, grow strong through this moving, having seen their own strength, and weakness; and if they are white men, tremble, curse, and go mad, because they will be drenched with the filth of their evil.

Tradition in African American Writing

The statement is at once descriptive and prescriptive, not unlike [ancient Greek philosopher] Aristotle's *Poetics* which is both a description of the practice of leading Greek playwrights of his day and a recommendation or prescription to future playwrights. Except for the anticipated effect of the work of art on the audience (and such effect is always a theoretical ideal and difficult to measure), Baraka's statement accurately describes the main tradition of Afro-American writing from the slave narratives and abolitionist fiction to the novels of [Richard] Wright, [Chester] Himes, and [Ralph] Ellison, the essays of [W.E.B.] Du Bois, [James] Baldwin, and [Eldridge] Cleaver, and the poetry and drama of the Black Consciousness era of the 1960s and 70s. Certainly, it describes Hughes's lifelong artistic theory and practice....

Hughes's "report" includes a picture of America as a cage, a zoo, a circus, a gory monster cannibal and a syphilitic whore, and the black man as deracinated, alienated, exiled, groping for reconnection with his African past. Africa is "time lost," surviving only in fragments and in dim racial memories felt, like the music that is its chief surrogate, in the blood and bones, in received culture not fully understood. Hughes was more fortunate than most of his contemporaries in that he had actually visited the coastal areas of West Africa, a region rich in history for Afro-Americans....

What is crucial is not so much Hughes's image of Africa as his image of America. In his early poems, Africa is for him a distant ideal, foil and backdrop for his portrait of the present reality that is America. America to him is a cold, joyless wilderness, Africa a carefree tropical paradise, a land where it would be customary, for instance, to "work maybe a little today, rest a little tomorrow. Play awhile. Sing awhile. O, let's dance." Uprooted from a natural environment of palms and forests and silver moons, blacks in America suffocate in a prison of skyscrapers and industrial smog. And as lions, tigers, and elephants, nature's majestic creatures created to live free, are trapped and harnessed for entertainment and profit, so have the nonwhite peoples of the world been converted from human beings into natural resources in the Western "circus of civilization."

Forced to play "the dumb clown of the world," the black man finds a limited victory in laughter, hiding his "tears and sighs" (to use [poet Paul Laurence] Dunbar's phrase) behind a mask that "grins and lies." The comic exterior is the black entertainer's particular stereotype. Hughes himself muffles a blazing rage behind his genial mask. But in "Summer Night" and "Disillusion," in the solitude of privacy, the public mask is momentarily lifted, and we feel in full the anguish of the poet or his persona. Like the rest of his brethren trapped in this circus, he tosses weary and sleepless, his soul "empty as the silence." The mask, the music, the wild laughter of Harlem's nights are but temporary escapes. And he longs for a return to the wholeness both of childhood and of the African past:

> I would be simple again,
>
> Simple and clean
>
> Like the earth,
>
> Like the rain. . . . . . .

Hope in the Face of Pain

The "Proem," later titled "Negro," which introduces *The Weary Blues*, is both a catalogue of wrongs against the black man over the centuries and a celebration of the strength by which he has survived those wrongs. That strength, a strength rooted in hope where there is no visible basis for hope, is . . . the essence of the blues. Outside of the blues, its most profound expressions in Hughes's poetry are in "Mother to Son," "The Negro Mother," "I, Too," and "The Negro Speaks of Rivers."

Mother to Son

Well, son, I'll tell you:

Life for me ain't been no crystal stair.

It's had tacks in it,

And splinters,

And boards torn up,

And places with no carpet on the floor—

Bare.

But all the time

I'se been a-climbin' on,

And reachin' landin's,

And turnin' corners,

And sometimes goin' in the dark

Where there ain't been no light.

So boy, don't you turn back.

Don't you set down on the steps

'Cause you finds it's kinder hard.

Don't you fall now—

For I'se still goin', honey,

I'se still climbin',

And life for me ain't been no crystal stair.

"The Negro Mother" is a narrative version (dramatic monologue) of the more compact and earlier "Mother to Son." Both poems share the metaphor of life as a journey, in particular a climbing up the ladder of success, or "up the great stairs" to heaven's golden gate. For the rich, the stairs are crystal and smooth and the climb easy; for the poor, the stairs are splintered and torn up and dark, not unlike the ghetto stairway of "The Ballad of the Landlord," and the climb is slow and arduous. (Or: the rich ride up in elevators, but tenement dwellers must walk up.) To get to the top, one must keep moving, cannot stop and sit. "I *had* to keep on! No stopping for me." To stop is to become a sitter on stoops and stander on street corners (the ghetto versions of the beach bum), or to become a prostitute, pimp, hustler, or thief. To despair is, in short, to wither and die. And as one conscious of her destiny as bearer of "the seed of the Free," one therefore on whom the future depended, the Black Mother chose to keep climbing. This is her achievement, that she survived to bear and nourish new generations, a staggering achievement under the circumstances.... These men and women acquiesced in their own humiliation and kept climbing on in order to prepare the way for "the coming Free." Their reward is in their vision of the possibility of freedom for their children. They are conservers and transmitters of the national soul, an example of love, wisdom, perseverance, and triumph for the younger generations to emulate.

Both poems reflect the form of a church testimony, with the lesson: "It's a sin to give up. I'm pressing toward the mark." This along with the traditional religious image of the stairs, and the stark endurance, fuelled by the "dream like steel in my soul" and expressed in "a song and a prayer," show both poems as emerging from the same big sea as the traditional spirituals and blues.

The Future in America of the Black Race

I, Too

I, too, sing America.

I am the darker brother.

Race in the Poetry of Langston Hughes

W.E.B. Du Bois was an African American author and editor who cofounded the National Association for the Advancement of Colored People (NAACP). Langston Hughes was heavily influenced by the writing of Du Bois and dedicated his poem "The Negro Speaks of Rivers" to him. © Hulton Archive/Getty Images.

They send me to eat in the kitchen

When company comes,

But I laugh,

And eat well,

> And grow strong.
>
> Tomorrow,
>
> I'll sit at the table
>
> When company comes.
>
> Nobody'll dare
>
> Say to me
>
> "Eat in the kitchen,"
>
> Then.
>
> Besides,
>
> They'll see how beautiful I am
>
> And be ashamed,—
>
> I, too, am America.

"I, Too" is as stoical as it is affirmative. Hughes accepts the brotherhood of black and white as beyond question. In addition, white and mulatto are brothers by immediate blood. The "darker brother" is America's secret shame, the kitchen his secret kingdom.... He bides his time, eats well and grows strong, confident in his own beauty, and confident that "tomorrow" he will share the table (of communion) with the others. The domestic context lends mythic depth to the poem; for what we are witnessing is the career of the young prince dispossessed and suppressed by his wicked relatives. The certainty of his return and reinstatement is foretold in the archetypes.

The poem seems in particular response to Walt Whitman's insistent singing of his American soil and genealogy:

> My tongue, every atom of my blood, form'd from this
>
> soil, this air,

Born here of parents born here from parents the same,

and their parents the same....

The black man's roots in American soil are as deep, indeed deeper than the roots of most whites. Therefore Hughes, too, celebrates America, but unlike Whitman, not the America that is but the America that is to come. The democratic vistas which Whitman saw all about him are, to Hughes, still distant on the horizon, yet to be.

Hughes's Expression of Heritage and Soul

The Negro Speaks of Rivers

I've known rivers:

I've known rivers ancient as the world and older than the

flow of human blood in human veins.

My soul has grown deep like the rivers.

I bathed in the Euphrates when dawns were young.

I built my hut near the Congo and it lulled me to sleep.

I looked upon the Nile and raised the pyramids above it.

I heard the singing of the Mississippi when Abe Lincoln

went down to New Orleans, and I've seen its muddy

bosom turn all golden in the sunset.

I've known rivers:

Ancient, dusky rivers.

My soul has grown deep like the rivers.

"The Negro Speaks of Rivers" is perhaps the most profound of these poems of heritage and strength. Composed when Hughes was a mere 17 years old, and dedicated to W.E.B. Du Bois, it is a sonorous evocation of transcendent essences so ancient as to appear timeless, predating human existence, longer than human memory. The rivers are part of God's body, and participate in his immortality. They are the earthly analogues of eternity: deep, continuous, mysterious. They are named in the order of their association with black history. The black man has drunk of their life-giving essences, and thereby borrowed their immortality. He and the rivers have become one. The magical transformation of the Mississippi from mud to gold by the sun's radiance is mirrored in the transformation of slaves into free men by Lincoln's Proclamation (and, in Hughes's poems, the transformation of shabby cabarets into gorgeous palaces, dancing girls into queens and priestesses by the spell of black music). As the rivers deepen with time, so does the black man's soul; as their waters ceaselessly flow, so will the black soul endure. The black man has seen the rise and fall of civilizations from the earliest times, seen the beauty and death—changes of the world over the thousands of years, and will survive even this America. . . .

Lynching in the South

In describing America, Hughes pays particular attention to the South, for the obvious reason that the black man's un-freedom is most starkly evident there. The South with its lynchings is, in his view, the measure of America. In "Magnolia Flowers," the poet goes South looking for the region's storied beauty, but finds instead "a corner full of ugliness.". . .

The most prolonged and deeply moving of Hughes's lynch poems is "The Bitter River," a dirge for two black youths lynched in Mississippi in 1942. Hughes conceives of the lynch terror as a bitter, poisonous river flowing through the South, a river at which black people have been forced to drink too long. Its water galls the taste, poisons the blood, and drowns black hopes. The "snake-like hiss of its stream" strangles black dreams. The bitter river reflects no stars, only the steel bars behind which are confined numberless innocents—the Scottsboro Boys, sharecroppers, and labor leaders....

Hughes's most brilliant lynch poem is "Christ in Alabama," one of the four poems accompanying the title play in *Scottsboro Limited* (1932). The Scottsboro Boys, eight black youths falsely accused of rape on the forced testimony of [two] disreputable white women, were in jail awaiting a legal lynching. This was the occasion of Hughes's epigrammatic "Justice":

That Justice is a blind goddess

Is a thing to which we black are wise:

Her bandage hides two festering sores

That once perhaps were eyes.

In the poem "Scottsboro" the youths are identified with Jesus Christ, John Brown, Nat Turner, [Mahatma] Gandhi, and other martyrs. These men are not dead, Hughes declares, they are immortal; and "Is it much to die when immortal feet / March with you down Time's street ...?" In "Christ in Alabama" Jesus is pictured as a lynched black man:

Christ is a nigger,

Beaten and black:

Oh, bare your back!

Mary is His mother;

Mammy of the South,

Silence your mouth.

God is His father:

> White Master above
>
> Grant Him your love.
>
> Most holy bastard
>
> Of the bleeding mouth,
>
> Nigger Christ
>
> On the cross
>
> Of the South.

"Christ is a n-----" in two senses: in the historical sense as a brown-skinned Jew like other Jews of his day, with a brown-skinned mother—both later adopted into the white West and given a lily-white heavenly father; and in the symbolic sense of Jesus as an alien presence, preaching an exacting spirituality, a foreign religion as it were, much as the black man, with his different color and culture, is an alien presence in the South. Each is a scapegoat sacrificed for the society's sins....

Hughes Also Wrote Political Poetry

Through the four decades of his career Hughes's poetry reflected public concerns, borrowing insights from the spirit of each era. The 1930s and 60s were the particular decades of radicals and extremists, and for Hughes each was an ideological and rhetorical decade, the 30s perhaps more so than the 60s: the difference was between the fire and enthusiasm of a young man in his thirties and the weariness and disappointment of an old man in his sixties who finds his dreams still deferred.

Some of Hughes's political poetry of the 30s was collected in two pamphlets: *Scottsboro Limited* (1932) and *A New Song* (1938). Both are party-line statements calling for revolution, calling on black and white workers to sink their racial antagonisms and band together to overthrow their common enemy, the capitalist ruling class and its agents.

Langston Hughes + Poetry = The Blues

Yusef Komunyakaa

Yusef Komunyakaa is the Distinguished Senior Poet at New York University. Some of his collections of poetry include Neon Vernacular, *which won the Pulitzer Prize for Poetry;* Pleasure Dome; Warhorses; *and* The Chameleon Couch.

African American folktales, superstitions, music, and customs have had a significant influence on modern American art, including that of Langston Hughes. Hughes was struck by the musical form of the blues. His poetry reflects this musical style both in beat and verticalness. This blues-infused poetic form creates a tension and a sense of urgency with short lines. At the same time, his poetry mimics the improvisation of African American lives. Hughes speaks to the black community about happiness while looking to the future and forging a new black culture of art, music, and literature.

> And far into the night he crooned that tune.
>
> The stars went out and so did the moon.
>
> The singer stopped playing and went to bed.
>
> While the Weary Blues echoed through his head.

When we analyze and weigh the most innovative voices of the Harlem Renaissance, Langston Hughes—alongside Zora Neale Hurston, Jean Toomer, and Helene Johnson—remains at the axis. Where Countee Cullen and Claude McKay embraced the archaism of the Keatian ode and the Elizabe-

---

Yusef Komunyakaa, "Langston Hughes + Poetry = The Blues," *Callaloo*, vol. 4, 2002. Copyright © 2002 by Johns Hopkins University Press. All rights reserved. Reproduced by permission.

than sonnet,[1] respectively, Hughes grafted on to his modernist vision traditional blues as well as the Chicago Renaissance (Vachel Lindsay and Carl Sandburg).[2] So, as the other voices grew silent during the Great Depression of 1929—with modernism[3] and imagism[4] having taken a firm hold and reshaped the tongue and heart of American poetry—the 1930s found a prolific Hughes. From the outset an American-ness had been at the center of Hughes's work, which is one of the reasons he has endured. Even his benchmark poem "The Negro Speaks of Rivers" plumbs the "muddy bosom" of the Mississippi after its narrator praises the Euphrates and the Congo (i.e., after taking readers on a tour through African heritage, the poem focuses on racial tensions in America).

Like Walt Whitman, the pulse and throb of Hughes's vision is driven by an acute sense of beauty and tragedy in America's history. Arnold Rampersad says in *The Life of Langston Hughes* that "On a visit to Kansas City he became aware of yet another aspect of black culture on which he would draw later as an artist and an individual. At an open air theatre on Independence Avenue, from an orchestra of blind musicians, Hughes first heard the blues. The music seemed to cry, but the words somehow laughed." Where Whitman had embraced the aria of the Italian opera (horizontal music), Hughes's divining rod quivered over the bedrock of the blues (vertical music).[5] The short lines of the blues poems create a syncopated insistence and urgency. Art has to have tension. And it is the simultaneous laughter and crying that create the tension in Hughes's blues poetry.[6] Hughes writes in "Homesick Blues": "Homesick blues is / A terrible thing to have. / To keep from cryin' / I opens ma mouth an' laughs."

In "Midwinter Blues" we find the same tension:

Don't know's I'd mind his goin'

But he left me when the coal was low.

Don't know's I'd mind his goin'

But he left when the coal was low.

Now, if a man loves a woman

That ain't no time to go.

Hughes also incorporates a jagged lyricism and modulation into his poetry by using short lines—a modern feeling that depends on a vertical movement that sidesteps contemplation but invites action/motion. There is confrontation in the blues. Stephen Henderson states in *Understanding the New Black Poetry*: "In oral tradition, the dogged determination of the work songs, the tough-minded power of the blues, the inventive energy of jazz, and the transcendent vision of God in the spirituals and the sermons, all energize the idea of Freedom, of Liberation, which is itself liberated from the temporal, the societal, and the political."

Hughes seems to have set out to take poetry off the page and toss it up into the air we breathe; he desired to bring poetry into our daily lives. In essence, he wanted his blues chants to parallel the improvisation in the lives of African Americans:

To fling my arms wide

In the face of the sun.

Dance! Whirl! Whirl!

Till the quick day is done.

Rest at pale evening . . .

A tall, slim tree . . .

Night coming tenderly

Black like me.

Hughes speaks here about daring joy to enter black life. The poem, "Dream Variations" is more than the speaker daydreaming about bringing images of nature into Harlem (the first black metropolis of the modern world): this is celebration and revolution in the same breath. Hughes addresses the future, forging through imagery and metaphor, the possibility of a new black culture in literature, music, and the arts.

To date, Amiri Baraka is one of the first names that light on the tongue if one were to ask, Who is the rightful heir to the Langston Hughes Legacy? This is mainly due to his long allegiance to jazz and the blues through essays and poetry. But, some would argue that his most successful poems are informed by his Black Mountain School[7] connection (the poems in *The Dead Lecturer* are touched by a blues feeling). He says in his "Blues, Poetry, and the New Music" essay that "I begin with blues because it is the basic national voice of the African American people. It is the fundamental verse form (speech, dance, verse/song) and musical form of the African American slave going through successive transformations."[8] Undoubtedly, Baraka owes much to Hughes, as do many other voices—black and white. But some would say, What about Sherley Anne Williams? Just mentioning her name is enough to almost bring Hughes to life; her tribute to Bessie Smith underlines what Hughes was striving for in the blues idiom:

> She was looking in
>
> my mouth and I knowed
>
> no matter what words
>
> come to my mind the
>
> song'd be her'n jes as
>
> well as it be mine.

Sherley Anne Williams receives my vote. But one of the most recent voices associated with Hughes is Willie Perdomo. Claude Brown's blurb on the cover of Perdomo's book of verse, *Where a Nickel Costs a Dime* (the title is a Hughes line), proclaims the following: "Langston Hughes has been reincarnated and lives in Spanish Harlem." True, some of the same anger is there; true, most of Perdomo's lines are short, with a similar jagged rhythm that is often linked to the blues; true, the urban subject matter might force the reader or listener to think of Hughes's simplicity with that which is simple. Yet Hughes's poetry is rather complex because it filters through the lenses of insinuation and satire. The laughter fuses with the crying, and the synthesis is affirmation. This is what Albert Murray seems to address in *The Blue Devils of Nada*:

> As for the blues statement, regardless of what it reflects, what it *expresses* is a sense of life that is affirmative. The blues lyrics reflect that which they confront, of course, which includes the absurd, the unfortunate, and the catastrophic; but they also reflect the person making the confrontation, his self-control, his sense of structure and style; and they express, among other things, his sense of humor as well as his sense of ambiguity and his sense of possibility. Thus, the very existence of the blues tradition is irrefutable evidence that those who evolved it respond to the vicissitudes of the human condition not with hysterics and desperation but through the wisdom of poetry informed by pragmatic insight.

Notes

1. Cullen modeled his poetry on the verse of the nineteenth-century British poet John Keats; McKay's models were the seventeenth-century Elizabethan poets, including William Shakespeare.

2. According to Hughes's biographer, Faith Berry, Hughes's high school English teacher (at Central High in Cleveland), "introduced her class to the Chicago school of poets: Vachel Lindsay, Edgar Lee Masters, and—the poet Hughes admired most, and eventually his greatest influence in the matter of form—Carl Sandburg."

3. Modernist poets like T.S. Eliot, Wallace Stevens, and Ezra Pound broke away from poetic traditions of the nineteenth century, such as rhyme and "flowery" lan-

guage, the kind of poetry Cullen and Claude McKay continued to write.

4. Imagism was a post–World War I literary movement that rebelled against nineteenth-century Romanticism and promoted the use of free verse and precise, concentrated imagery. The early poems of William Carlos Williams and the poetry of H.D. exemplify this tradition.

5. The lines of Whitman's verse are very long, giving his poetry a horizontal feel. Hughes's lines are short, so the reader's eyes move quickly down the page, giving the poetry a sense of verticalness.

6. In a review of W.C. Handy's *Blues: An Anthology* Langston Hughes says the blues grew out of "the racial hurt and the racial ecstasy," out of "trouble with incongruous overtones of laughter [and] joy with strange undertones of pain."

7. The Black Mountain School refers to an artists' colony in North Carolina with which Baraka was associated during the 1950s.

8. Hughes said much the same thing about jazz.

Langston Hughes: The Writer, His Poetics and the Artistic Process[1]

Martha Cobb

Martha Cobb (d. 2010) was the author of twenty articles in scholarly journals. She was professor of Spanish at Howard University and was instrumental in establishing Afro-Hispanic studies at Howard.

Langston Hughes was one of the first African American writers to unapologetically merge his voice with racial oral history, "to express our dark-skinned selves without fear or shame," he wrote in 1926. He subsequently would work in a variety of genres but never lose his black point of reference. In one of his first and most famous poems, he connects the history of his race with his own soul, using the image of a river traveling through history. One of Hughes's poems, in the voice of his grandmother, relates her lifelong problems but also her consistent hope—"I'se still climbin.'" Some of his other poems echo African American spirituals and the need of the blues to sooth misery. Hughes proposes black speech, rhythms, and themes as means to liberation for the oppressed and as ways to express the values of the race.

Literary art represents the qualities of excellence, truth and values that a society discerns and conveys in the expressive forms which it chooses for representing itself, inclusive of beginnings as humble as spirituals, blues folk stories and slave narratives that are embedded in the black experience of life and are reflected in its art. It bears repeating that the beginnings of African-American literatures, in whatever country of the African diaspora they are found to be located, were created within the framework of black oral traditions with their own contextual and stylistic variations based on what the voice and the spirit have to say, to sing about, and pass on to the next generation. Representative writers in the twentieth century—and one can certainly start with W.E.B. Du Bois—have interpreted, reproduced, and assimilated traditional black forms of expression and thought into an ongoing black literary tradition.

It is out of the traditions of these inherited patterns of black expression that Langston Hughes pioneered, using his creative imagination to transform the intrinsic nature of black verbal art to a poetic literature whose aesthetic character altered the consciousness of audiences and fellow poets alike. Among the latter, Nicolás Guillén of Cuba and Jacques Roumain of Haiti represent the confluent streams of what can be designated a Langston Hughes tradition.

The Writer. Born in Joplin, Missouri, in 1902, Langston Hughes' first published poem "The Negro Speaks of Rivers" appeared in the *Crisis* magazine in June 1921, foreshadowing the direction of his later literary art. By 1926 Hughes had moved to New York City where the publication of *The Weary Blues* confirmed the emergence of two aspects that were to inform the growth and character of black literature, namely: the larger and earthier stream of black oral traditions that would be shaped on the printed page, by the creative imagination of the poet-writer's individual talent. This converging of the traditional stream of black speech, black story, black folk forms with Hughes' poetic sensibility as individual poet-writer enabled the then young author to find his cultural base, which he underscored when he announced in 1926—asserting himself with the flourish and fanfare of the new young poet claiming his place in the pantheon and challenging his elders: "We younger writers who create now intend to express our individual dark-skinned selves without fear or shame. If white people are pleased we are glad. If they are not, it doesn't matter. We know we are beautiful. And ugly, too. If colored people are pleased we are glad. If they are not their displeasure doesn't matter either. We build our temples for tomorrow, strong as we know how, and we stand on top of the mountain, free within ourselves."[2]

Remarkable for the time in which this statement was issued, it clearly defines Hughes, the man and the literary artist. In subsequent published works, Langston Hughes was to experiment in the writing of other literary genres in prose, in writing for the stage, but he never deviated, in his long career, from the centrality of the black point of view nor from the artistic process that enabled him to elicit the fundamental qualities of oral folk expression from his vision and valuation of black life.

If questions were to be raised—what makes a black writer? How does he or she achieve the qualities of excellence in style and thought which an audience admires and responds to?—the answers surely lie in the quality of telling the truth, in the commitment to the values of the people he represents. In Hughes' case, the character of his poetry and prose lies in the black points of reference that his works reveal, in the employment of rhythmic black forms of expression to tell the story of the people, in his merging of the personal-artistic-black point of view to create effects for evoking responses to his poetry, and for locating his poetry at a point where reality and imagination meet and share a common meaning. The answers may vary, but for Hughes the combination of psychology, reality, and creative imagination kept him close to the thought and emotional thrust of the audiences for whom he wrote. Thus, in the quest for art forms that would best represent his heritage, Hughes attempted to translate what he saw and heard on the streets of Harlem, in the hustle of New York life, in churches and dance halls, into verbal and thematic patterns that celebrated black life, black survival, the color black, black

Langston Hughes was especially inspired by jazz and blues music, spending hours in the nightclubs of Harlem, New York, listening and writing. © Markus Amon/Getty Images.

pride, and black humor. Moreover, in the quality of the styles he initiated, Langston Hughes, the artist-writer was able to evoke the essential reality of black men and women, a reality made meaningful through verbal art forms that appear in a diversity of patterns in his poetry, in his dramas, and in his stories.

The Poetics. Langston Hughes is a significant figure in American literature because his authorial presence in the twentieth century merged "individual talent"—to use T.S. Eliot's term—with the traditional "souls of black folk," to employ the title and the substance of W.E.B. Du Bois' famous book, first published in 1903. The souls that Du Bois described so movingly in his work become the tradition that Langston Hughes drew upon to achieve the aesthetic effects of black life, black speech, black music which, according to writer-critic Stephen Henderson,[3] are central to presentations out of which what I am calling a black *poetics* can be defined.

In considering the poetics of Langston Hughes, I am talking about expressive style, creative imagination, and aesthetic character, each of which is intrinsic to the working out of literary patterns that originated in the oral traditions of a people. The style of presentation, therefore, is a very individual technique for presenting the reality one perceives through the structures of culture and language that give meaning to the *stuff of life* according to one's angle of vision. This, I suggest, is the "talent" of Langston Hughes, the "poetic" from which his style has developed and which allows him to interpret, with the precision of poetic techniques, what he perceives from a personal, black point of view. If any one element stands out in the structuring of his "poetic" through traditional black expressive forms, it is the element of *voice* which constantly projects a black observer, black speaker within the framework of the black experience of life. A few examples of *voice* within the structure that has been described will suffice:

> I've known rivers:
>
> I've known rivers ancient as the world and older than the
>
> flow of human blood in human veins.
>
> My soul has grown deep like the rivers.[4]

Or, the black mother or grandmother attempting to raise her child under the most negative circumstances,

> Well, son I'll tell you:
>
> Life for me ain't been no crystal stair.
>
> It's had tacks in it,
>
> And splinters,
>
> And boards torn up,
>
> And places with no carpet on the floor—
>
> Bare.

. . . .

    Don't you fall now—

    For I'se still goin', honey,

    I'se still climbin',

    And life for me ain't been no crystal stair.[5]

And one with undertones of the black spiritual:

    At the feet o' Jesus,

    Sorrow like a sea.

    Lordy, let yo' mercy

    Come driftin' down on me.

    At the feet o' Jesus

    At yo' feet I stand.

    O, ma little Jesus,

    Please reach out yo' hand.[6]

Or here, the tight poetic pattern of the blues, with the first line repeated and a third line to carry the statement forward, followed by a concluding statement that usually rhymes with the statement of the first two lines:

    Play the blues for me

    Play the blues for me

    No other music

    'Ll ease my misery.

    Sing a soothin' song.

    Said a soothin' song,

    Cause the man I love's done

    Done me wrong.

. . . .

Black gal like me

Black gal like me

'S got to hear a blues

For her misery.[7]

Coming from the least privileged segments of the black community, art and life intersect in a verbal transaction that can move from blues to spirituals to the wry humor of Jesse B. Semple, establishing the sense of a true black consciousness of self and of a people that not only maintains its own dignity but that somehow liberates itself from that which is mean and ugly and defeated. Hughes' use of black ways of expression, of handling black speech, black rhythms, black themes, lifts the meanings of words out of their negative contexts and places them in the broader and deeper stream of poetic art. Stated from a critical perspective, Hughes has illustrated black values, focused on black thought and its expressive modes by defining the *voice* of a people.

The Artistic Process. The term *process* is used here to sum up the relation of the individual author to the development of a historically authenticated literary tradition, and within that tradition the evolution of styles that serve to carry forward themes out of the black experiences of life. At this point it should be clear that Langston Hughes as individual author is both a carrier and creator of the artistic processes on a scale broad enough to replicate oral traditions, to recreate imaginative patterns from the voice of the folk that make Afro-American verbal art a strong and distinctive literature. The artistic process, then, assumes language patterns and aesthetic forms that communicate a shared black experience, and underlying it, the deeply rooted traditions of black folklore as they are introduced into the written word by perceptive writers within a culture. Thus folklore itself is a process, handed down through language communication that is primarily oral:

a dynamic, changing mode of communication obeying its own artistic principles, and ultimately subsumed by the perceptive artists of the printed word.

This, then, is the artistic process by which much, if not most, of the best black literature can be identified, and which defines the importance of Langston Hughes and other black writers like him. For as surely as black folk forms, their modes of expression, and their themes in the United States enter into the stream of written literature, so the artistic process holds true in other countries of the African diaspora. Thus Nicolás Guillén in Cuba and Jacques Roumain in Haiti, both of whom Langston Hughes knew personally, whom he translated into English, and whom he inspired to go to folk sources, need to be studied for the confluence of black folkloric contributions they have made to the printed Afro-Hispanic and Afro-French literature in the Americas.

To understand black literature and to interpret it intelligently, and in depth, it is of primary importance to examine the artistic process of which folklore is one—but probably the strongest and most integral element—that represents the true black reality at a particular developmental stage of black literature, its writers, and its poetics.

Notes

1. This paper was presented at the College Language Association's Convention in Philadelphia, Pennsylvania, on Friday, April 22, 1983, in a symposium sponsored by the Langston Hughes Society entitled "Harlem, Haiti, and Havana: The Pioneer Confluence of a Hughesonian Tradition."
2. Langston Hughes, "The Negro Artist and the Racial Mountain," *The Nation* (June 23, 1926), 694.
3. Stephen Henderson, *Understanding the New Black Poetry* (New York: William Morrow and Company, Inc., 1973), p. 3.

4. "The Negro Speaks of Rivers," from *Selected Poems of Langston Hughes* (New York: Alfred A. Knopf, 1959), p. 4.
5. *Ibid.*, "Mother to Son," p. 187.
6. *Ibid.*, "Feet o' Jesus," p. 17.
7. *Ibid.*, "Misery," p. 143.

Hughes's Contradictory Reactions to the Christian Church

Mary Beth Culp

Mary Beth Culp, a teacher at Marymount College in California, has written on ragtime, Langston Hughes, and African American religion. She has written reviews for the Los Angeles Times.

Langston Hughes is fundamentally a social poet of his race, and a substantial—defining—part of the African American social experience. Hughes was influenced by religion and the church, and he wrote more than sixty poems touching on religion. Religion has been a source of strength and comfort for the oppressed, a point of view that can be seen in Hughes's poems about the person of Jesus and the poem "Judgment Day." Religion and the African American church, however, have also been obstacles to emancipation, manhood, and reform. The religious institution keeps the African American docile. The white church has also used religion to justify slavery and segregation. Churches in some areas were the last institutions to fight integration. In one particularly provocative poem, Hughes asserts that socialism and communism will save the poor—not Christianity.

Langston Hughes lived basically in terms of the external world and in unison with it, making himself one with his people and refusing to stand apart as an individual. His poetry reflects collective states of mind as if they were his own, merging the poet's personality with his racial group. He assumes various personae—sometimes he is the spirit of his race, at other times he is a spittoon polisher, a black mother, a

---

Mary Beth Culp, "Religion in the Poetry of Langston Hughes," *Phylon*, vol. 48, no. 3, Fall 1987, pp. 240–245. Copyright © 1987 by Phylon and Clark Atlanta University. All rights reserved. Reproduced by permission.

prostitute, a black man without job or money—but there is a commonality among the various experiences presented in his poems which gives them a kind of consistent persona.

Religion as Integral to African American Culture

As a folklorist Hughes sought to capture the essence of every aspect of black culture, including its religion. Religious feeling is always interdependent with racial feeling in his poetry. He views religion in the larger context of black culture, presenting it variously as a source of strength for the oppressed, an opiate of the people, the religion of slavery, and an obstacle to emancipation. When asked in an interview about his own religious views, Hughes responded:

> I grew up in a not very religious family, but I had a foster aunt who saw that I went to church and Sunday School . . . and I was very much moved, always, by the, shall I say, the rhythms of the Negro church . . . of the spirituals . . . of those wonderful old-time sermons. . . . There's great beauty in the mysticism of much religious writing, and great help there—but I also think that we live in a world . . . of solid earth and vegetables and a need for jobs and a need for housing. . .

In the only poem in which Hughes speaks of religion in his own voice and not that of a persona of his people, he states:

In an envelope marked:

Personal

God addressed me a letter.

In an envelope marked:

Personal

I have given my answer.

In the remainder of his more than sixty poems containing religious references, Hughes captures the essence of religious feeling in the black culture through his use of language, rhythm, and form. The simplest of these is a group of six lyrics and songs composed between 1926 and 1964, celebrating the story of the Christ Child. Another group, including "Judgment Day" (1927); "Prayer Meeting" (1923); "Sinner" (1927) and "Acceptance" (1957) reflect the simple faith of blacks in settings reminiscent of Hughes' childhood experiences. "Judgment Day" dramatizes the imagination of a simple black person whose soul has gone "flyin' to de stars and moon / A shoutin' God I's comin' soon!"

Among Hughes' poems which suggest that religion has been valuable to black people in toughening a certain life force within, one of the most popular is "The Negro Mother" (1931). The archetypal speaker says:

> I am the one who labored as a slave, Beaten and mistreated for the work that I gave ... Three hundred years in the deepest South: But God put a song and a prayer in my mouth. God put a dream like steel in my soul.

Here the religion of the slave masters has become resolution in the mind of the slaves....

Perhaps the most powerful of Hughes' poems with a religious reference, however, are those which use Christ as a central figure. In the poetry of Hughes, as well as other black poets, Christ is sometimes white, symbolizing the oppressors and acting as their accomplice; at other times he is black, the image and friend of the lynched Negro, and one who suffers with him. With the black-white Christ symbol black poets have represented the contradictory elements of the religion of whites which was passed on to the slaves.

The Religion of the Oppressor

In the original version of "A New Song" (1932) the poet expresses regret that the Negro has never really shared in the

Christian community; he denies that Christ's sacrifice took place on behalf of black people, and asserts that the blacks must redeem themselves.

> Bitter was the day
>
> When . . .
>
> . . . only in the sorrow songs
>
> Relief was found—
>
> Yet no relief,
>
> But merely humble life and silent death
>
> Eased by a Name
>
> That hypnotized the pain away—
>
> O, precious Name of Jesus in that day!
>
> That day is past.
>
> I know full well now
>
> Jesus could not die for me
>
> That only my own hands,
>
> Dark as the earth,
>
> Can make my earth-dark body free.

"Goodbye Christ" (1933) spurns the Christ of white supremacy and reflects an attraction to Communist ideology, although Hughes later declared he had never shared the views expressed in this poem.

> Listen, Christ,
>
> You did alright in your day, I reckon—
>
> But that day's gone now.
>
> They ghosted you up a swell story, too,
>
> Called it Bible—

> But it's dead now.
>
> The popes and the preachers've
>
> Made too much money from it.
>
> They've sold you to too many
>
> Kings, generals, robbers, and killers—
>
> . . .
>
> Goodbye,
>
> Christ Jesus Lord God Jehova,
>
> Beat it on away from here now.
>
> Make way for a new guy with no religion at all—
>
> A real guy named
>
> Marx Communist Lenin Peasant Stalin Worker ME.

As a result of this poem, the poet was barred from speaking at a Los Angeles YMCA in 1935, was picketed by the America First Party while speaking at Wayne State University in 1942, and fifteen years later was still explaining that the poem was an "ironic protest against racketeering in the churches."

Jesus as an Archetype of Suffering Blacks

In other poems, Christ is seen as the archetype of suffering blacks. A comparison between the fate of Jesus and the revilement of black people appears in Hughes' poetry both early and late. In "Ma Lord" (1927) an anthropomorphic Christ is pictured. The second stanza reads:

> Ma Lord knowed what it was to work
>
> He knowed how to pray

Race in the Poetry of Langston Hughes

Fearing a mob lynching, Alabama governor B.M. Miller called the National Guard to the Scottsboro jail to protect the young black men who were accused of raping two white women. From left to right, the accused are Clarence Norris, Olen Montgomery, Andy Wright, Willie Roberson, Ozie Powell, Eugene Williams, Charlie Weems, Roy Wright, and Haywood Patterson. © Bettmann/Corbis.

Ma Lord's life was trouble, too
Trouble ever day.

The fusion of Christ and black people has a long tradition, reinforced by the influence of black ministers who drew comparisons between Christ's martyrdom and the debasement of black people. In his short story "Big Meeting" Hughes describes a typical sermon in which this identification is apparent. The sermon on the Crucifixion is divided into three parts. In the first, the preacher talks about the power of the lowly, represented by Christ; then about the ability of a man to stand alone like Jesus, who told his weakening disciples to "sleep on." The congregation chants, "sleep on, sleep on." The second part of the sermon turns to images of violence. The minister recalls that Jesus "saw the garden alive with men carrying lanterns and swords and staves, and the mob was every-

69

where." Other images of violence which the preacher supplies are *handcuffs, prisoner, chains, trail, lies*. Then the minister closes the gap between Christ and the congregation. The picture of the crucified Jesus is finished:

> Mob cussin' and hootin' my Jesus! Umn!
>
> The spit of the mob in His face! Umn!
>
> His body hangin' on the cross! Umn!
>
> . . .
>
> That's what they did to my Jesus!
>
> They stoned Him first, they stoned Him!
>
> Called Him everything but a child of God.
>
> Then they lynched him on the cross.

The word *mob* begins the Negro identification with Christ; the word *lynched* seals it. The sermon is almost a poem itself. In it one can see the "rhythms of the Negro church" to which Hughes referred in the interview cited.

The poem which is the strongest statement of this theme is "Christ in Alabama" (1931).

> Christ is a nigger,
>
> Beaten and black
>
> Oh, bare your back!
>
> Mary is His mother:
>
> Mammy of the South,
>
> Silence your mouth.
>
> God is His father:
>
> White Master above
>
> Grant Him your love.
>
> Most holy bastard

Of the bleeding mouth,
Nigger Christ
On the cross
Of the South.

Racial Cruelty and Protest Behind the Poetry

Hughes' first reading of the poem at the University of North Carolina on November 21, 1931, caused threats of violence from whites. The poem itself was written to protest violence against blacks which was weighing heavily on Hughes' mind. While on his reading tour of the South, he had learned that a recent graduate of Hampton Institute had been beaten to death by an Alabama mob for parking his car in a white parking lot. In the same week, he learned of the death of Juliette Derricotte of Fisk University, who had been involved in an automobile accident in Georgia and had been refused treatment in a white hospital. In addition, the Scottsboro case had affected Hughes deeply. Nine Negro youths were in Kilby prison in Alabama, accused of raping two white prostitutes in a coal car traveling through the state. In his autobiography *I Wonder as I Wander*, Hughes describes these events and their repercussions in his typical low-key, wry manner. He relates the reaction of a local politician in Chapel Hill to the poem: "It's bad enough to call Christ a bastard ... but to call Him a n------— that's too much!" In an article in the *Atlanta World* of December 18, 1931, Hughes said of the poem:

> Anything which makes people think of existing evil conditions is worthwhile. Sometimes in order to attract attention somebody must embody these ideas in sensational forms. I meant my poem to be a protest against the domination of all stronger peoples over weaker ones....

Perhaps Hughes' finest poem using the Crucifixion theme is "Song for a Dark Girl," written in 1927.

Way Down South in Dixie

(Break the heart of me)

They hung my black young lover

To a cross roads tree.

Way Down South in Dixie

(Bruised body high in air)

I asked the white Lord Jesus

What was the use of prayer.

Way Down South in Dixie

(Break the Heart of me)

Love is a naked shadow

On a gnarled and naked tree.

In this poem, protest has given way to grief. The irony of the gay Dixieland tune juxtaposed on the heartbreaking refrain gives the poem impact, as does its simple imagery and symbolism. In the first stanza, the black young lover is the Christ figure, hung to a *cross roads* (divided for emphasis) tree. In the second stanza, the speaker addresses the white Christ, expressing the frustration of the black religious experience in America. In the third stanza, the two Christ figures, representing love, are fused into "a naked shadow / On a gnarled and naked tree."

In these poems, as in all his works, Langston Hughes' primary purpose was to reveal the folk expression of his people in all its diversity. He shows the folk inside and outside the church, happy and sad, in states of grace and of sin. Although he wrote with emotional strength of the oppression of his people, he was primarily a folklorist who created his art out of the stuff of common black experience.

The Parental Rejection of the Tragic Mulatto

Arthur P. Davis

Arthur P. Davis (d. 1996) was an English professor at Howard University who authored Isaac Watts: His Life and Works *and edited* Cavalcade: Negro American Writing from 1760 to the Present. *Davis was a friend of Langston Hughes.*

The mulatto is usually portrayed in literature as a character with a white father and an African American (slave) mother and is stereotyped as one who has the intellectuality of the white father and the passion of the black mother. For Langston Hughes this was a topic of lifelong interest, and critics of Hughes have speculated that the figure resonated with his own life. In one poem on the subject, a male mulatto hates his wealthy father as well as his poor mother. He considers that the life of the mulatto will always be miserable. Although Hughes's father was an African American, the elder Hughes disliked his race and abandoned the young Hughes and his mother. Hughes's poems on the subject turn more and more bitter over time. The real evil is not the sexual union of black and white but the parental rejection by both father and mother.

*T*he Weary Blues (1926), the first publication of Langston Hughes, contained a provocative twelve-line poem entitled "Cross," which dealt with the tragic mulatto theme.... For over a quarter of a century, the author has been concerned with this theme; returning to it again and again, he has presented the thesis in four different genres, in treatments varying in length from a twelve-line poem to a full-length Broadway play.

Arthur P. Davis, "The Tragic Mulatto Theme in Six Works of Langston Hughes," *Phylon*, vol. 16, no. 2, Fall 1955, pp. 195–199, 203–204. Copyright © 1955 by Phylon and Clark Atlanta University. All rights reserved. Reproduced by permission.

Mulatto as a Type

Before discussing Mr. Hughes' several presentations of the theme, however, let us understand the term "tragic mulatto." As commonly used in American fiction and drama, it denotes a light-colored, mixed-blood character (possessing in most cases a white father and a colored mother), who suffers because of difficulties arising from his biracial background. In our literature there are, of course, valid and convincing portrayals of this type; but as it is a character which easily lends itself to sensational exaggeration and distortion, there are also many stereotypes of the tragic mulatto to be found. And these stereotypes, as Professor [Sterling A.] Brown has so ably pointed out, are not only marked by "exaggeration and omission"; they often embody racial myths and shibboleths. In them "the mulatto is a victim of divided inheritance; from his white blood come his intellectual strivings, his unwillingness to be a slave; from his Negro blood come his baser emotional urges, his indolence, his savagery." Whether any given character is a true flesh and blood portrait or a stereotype depends, of course, upon the knowledge, the skill, and the integrity of the artist; and this is true whether the author be Negro or white. But it would not be unfair to state that though both are guilty, the white writer tends to use the stereotype more often than the Negro.

Regardless of the approach, however—valid portrayal or stereotype—the tragic mulatto, because of our racial situation, has been popular with the American writer from the very beginnings of our literature.... Considering its popularity, we are not surprised that Langston Hughes has made use of the theme, but we are intrigued by the persistency with which he has clung to it over the years.

Why then has he been so deeply concerned with the tragic mulatto? Has he given us a deeper and more realistic analysis of the mixed-blood character? Are his central figures different from the stereotypes created by other writers? Or, does

Hughes, perhaps unconsciously, employ the theme of the tragic mulatto to express vicariously and symbolically some basic inner conflict in his own personality?...

Let us turn ... to "Cross," the original statement of the theme and the "germ-idea" from which the mulatto group was derived. Surprisingly stark and unadorned, the poem begins with ballad-like abruptness:

> My old man's a white old man
>
> And my old mother's black,
>
> If ever I cursed my white old man
>
> I take my curses back.
>
> If I ever cursed my black old mother
>
> And wished she were in hell,
>
> I am sorry for that evil wish
>
> And now I wish her well.
>
> My old man died in a fine big house,
>
> My ma died in a shack,
>
> I wonder where I'm gonna die,
>
> Being neither white nor black?

Through suggestion and implication rather than by direct narrative, the poet has given us in three quatrains the whole tragic story of a mulatto's bitter resentment against his "mixed" background and his failure in life which he seems to attribute to that background. We are told specifically that the mulatto at first blamed both parents for his plight; that subsequently, for some unstated reason, he forgives his father and mother; and finally that he pities himself because of a sense of not belonging. These are the stated facts of the piece, but a close reading of the poem suggests other implications as important as the facts themselves.

There is first of all the idea of desertion on the part of the white father indicated in the two separate death places—one in "a fine big house," the other in a shack. There is also rejection implied in that we assume the mulatto lived with his mother. We therefore detect a hint of envy and regret when he speaks of his father's inaccessible fine big house. Perhaps there is a bit of fondness on the part of the mulatto unconsciously expressed in the phrase "my old man." We know that he forgave his father, and we sense a feeling of regret on his part even for the death of a parent who had rejected him and whom he could not know. In the final analysis, the poem boils down to a fruitless search for a father and a home, and it is this pattern which Langston Hughes has followed in all of the subsequent works on the tragic mulatto theme.

In contrast to the classic restraint and economy of phrase we find in "Cross," Mr. Hughes in "Mulatto" writes with an exuberance which is almost hysterical in quality. We feel immediately the passion and violence, and we somehow get the impression that all of the speakers in the poem (it is a dramatic dialogue) are either shouting or screaming. The clash between white father and rejected son is driven home from the very first line:

I am your Son, White Man!

Georgia dusk

And the turpentine woods,

One of the pillars of the temple fell.

You are my son!

Like hell!

The moon over the turpentine woods.

The southern night

Full of stars,

Great big yellow stars.

Juicy bodies

Of nigger wenches

Blue black

Against black fences.

O, you little bastard boy,

What's a body but a toy?

The scent of pine wood stings the soft night air.

What's the body of your mother?

Silver moonlight everywhere.

What's the body of your mother?

Sharp pine scent in the evening air.

A nigger night,

A nigger joy,

A little yellow

Bastard boy.

Naw, you ain't my brother.

Niggers ain't my brother.

Not ever.

Niggers ain't my brother.

Git on back there in the night,

You ain't white . . .

I am your son, white man . . .

Rejection of Mulatto by Both Whites and Blacks

We note at once that the rejection theme so vaguely suggested in "Cross" has become the central theme of this poem. All other issues are subordinate to it; and all of the images, sym-

Langston Hughes, foreground, shown in his boyhood hometown of Lawrence, Kansas, circa 1914. Hughes left Lawrence a year later to live with his mother in Lincoln, Illinois. Much of Hughes's poetry conveys the turmoil he felt about being "rejected" by an African American father who despised being black. © AP Photo.

bols, incidents, and background scenery serve but to accentuate and dramatize the basic thesis of rejection. For example, Hughes intensifies the denial of kinship by making it now into a two-generation refusal: both half-brother and father brutally rebuff the mulatto. The poem also makes use of ironic contrast to degrade the mulatto's circumstances of birth. Stressing the stinging scent of the pine wood—a smell associated with cleanliness, purity, and idyllic lovemaking—he creates of it an inverted and distorted symbol of the sordid act of copulation between "blue black" n----- wenches and fallen white pillars of the temple. The idea of ironic contrast is further implied when he associates the clean and crystal-like brilliance of the innumerable "great big yellow stars" with the many "yellow bastards" so carelessly conceived beneath their sparkling splendor. The slurring reference on the part of the whites to this kind of evening's fun as "n----- joy" and the whole barbecue-like abandon of the scene both stress and dramatize the irresponsible casualness of this type of frolicking in the Negro section "against black fences." The use of the preposition "against" heightens the insult. All of these things serve not only to highlight the rejection of the mulatto but in effect to furnish a rationale for it.

The most insulting of these slurring expressions in the mouths of the white speakers is the line thrice repeated in the poem: "What's the body of your mother?" This slur, the rankest form of "the dozens," degrades the rejection of the yellow bastard past all hope of reconcilement. Hence there is no hint of fondness or forgiveness here. The mulatto, no longer a vaguely unhappy misfit as in "Cross," has become in the eyes of the whites a pariah, a mongrel cur who can never be "recognized." The rejection here is sadistically final and decisive.

Hughes Places All Blame on the Father Figure

We note one curious approach in "Mulatto." Hughes seems to place no blame at all on the dusky women who take part in these "n----- nights." He seems to ignore entirely their burden of guilt. All of his castigation is aimed at the white pillars of the temple who can indulge in such orgies and then callously reject the issue of their evening's pleasure. Is the poet suggesting that the black women are helpless victims? That would be too unrealistic. What he probably implies here is simply this: that the nocturnal interracial lovemaking itself is not the essential evil. It is the rejection of parenthood on the part of the father which is the unforgivable crime. And in other works on this theme, ... he recognizes the economic pressures which motivate these black-white liaisons. ...

Hughes' Father Rejected His Own Race

In short, Hughes reduces his tragic mulatto problem to a father and son conflict, and for him the single all-important and transcending issue is rejection—personal rejection on the part of the father.

I am convinced that Langston Hughes felt very keenly on this whole matter of rejection, and I believe that a most revealing postscript to this discussion of father-son relationships may be found in his autobiography, *The Big Sea* (1940). In this work there is a chapter entitled simply "Father," in which Hughes has accounted for, it seems to me, several of the attitudes he portrays in his tragic mulattoes.

Coming from a split home, Langston Hughes did not get to know his father until he was seventeen, the latter having moved to Mexico after the family breakup. During all of his early years of frequent removals and hand-to-mouth living with his mother and other relatives, Hughes came to look upon his father, living "permanently" in Mexico, as the "one stable factor" in his life. "He at least stayed put," and to the young Langston this was an impressive achievement. Although his mother had told him that the senior Hughes was a "devil on wheels," he did not believe her. On the contrary, he created in his mind a heroic image of his father, picturing him as a "strong bronze cowboy in a big Mexican hat," living free in a country where there was no race prejudice.

And then at seventeen, Hughes met his father and went to live with him in Mexico. Disillusionment came quickly, followed by a reaction far more serious. He found that the elder Hughes was neither kind nor understanding. "As weeks went by," he writes, "I could think of less and less to say to my father. His whole way of living was so different from mine...." For the first time, the boy began to understand why his mother had left her husband; he wondered why she had married him in the first place; and most important of all he wondered why they had chosen to have him. "Now at seventeen," Langston Hughes tells us, "I began to be very sorry for myself.... I began to wish that I had never been born—not under such circumstances."

And then this unhappy, seventeen-year-old boy . . . contemplated suicide: "One day, when there was no one in the house but me," he writes, "I put the pistol to my head and held it there, loaded, a long time, and wondered if I would be any happier if I were to pull the trigger."

Subsequently, during a spell of serious illness, Langston Hughes' dislike of his father crystallized into something dangerously approaching fixation. "And when I thought of my father," he tells us, "I got sicker and sicker. I hated my father."

That last short sentence helps to explain for me Hughes' persistent concern with the tragic mulatto theme. In his handling of the theme he has found an opportunity to write out of his system, as it were, the deep feelings of disappointment and resentment that he himself felt as a "rejected" son.

Hughes Took Advantage of the Tension Between Style and Theme

Raymond Smith

Raymond Smith, best known for the article "Langston Hughes: Evolution of the Poetic Persona," is himself both a poet and artist who has written widely on Hughes and illustrated some of Hughes's poems.

During the Great Depression of the 1930s, Langston Hughes made the promise to himself to devote his writings not just to an artistic enclave of the Harlem Renaissance but also to working-class African Americans. He found himself in the situation, described by distinguished African American writer W.E.B. Du Bois, as always being two people, looking at himself through the eyes of others and trying to be "as little Negro and as much American as possible." To unite these two selves, Hughes took on the role of poet. Unlike the poet Walt Whitman who celebrated himself, Hughes celebrated his race; there is little personal in his poems. Instead, his is a social voice, the voice of the oppressed. Hughes clearly saw this doubleness in his trip to Africa, where, as an American with some white blood, he was never accepted as a true black man.

When the noted Senegalese poet and exponent of African negritude, Léopold Senghor, was asked in a 1967 interview "In which poems of our, American, literature [do] you find evidence of Negritude?" his reply was "Ah, in Langston Hughes; Langston Hughes is the most spontaneous as a poet

---

Raymond Smith, "Langston Hughes: Evolution of the Poetic Persona," *Langston Hughes: Critical Perspectives Past and Present*, ed. Henry Louis Gates Jr. and K.A. Appiah. New York: Amistad Press, 1993, pp. 120–130, 133. Copyright © 1987 by AMS Press, Inc. All rights reserved. Reproduced by permission.

and the blackest in expression!" Before his death in 1967, Hughes had published more than a dozen volumes of poetry, in addition to a great number of anthologies, translations, short stories, essays, novels, plays, and histories dealing with the spectrum of Afro-American life.

Hughes's Choice to Write About Race

Of the major black writers who first made their appearance during the exciting period of the 1920s commonly referred to as "the Harlem Renaissance," Langston Hughes was the most prolific and the most successful. As the Harlem Renaissance gave way to the [Great] Depression, Hughes determined to sustain his career as a poet by bringing his poetry to the people. At the suggestion of Mary McLeod Bethune, he launched his career as a public speaker by embarking on an extensive lecture tour of the South. As he wrote in his autobiography: "Propelled by the backwash of the 'Harlem Renaissance' of the early 'twenties, I had been drifting along pleasantly on the delightful rewards of my poems which seemed to please the fancy of kindhearted New York ladies with money to help young writers.... There was one other dilemma—how to make a living from *the kind of writing I wanted to do*.... I wanted to write seriously and as well as I knew how about the Negro people, and make *that* kind of writing earn me a *living*." The Depression forced Hughes to reconsider the relation between his poetry and his people: "I wanted to continue to be a poet. Yet sometimes I wondered if I was barking up the wrong tree. I determined to find out by taking poetry, *my* poetry, to *my* people. After all, I wrote about Negroes, and primarily *for* Negroes. Would they have me? Did they want me?..."

The Black Poet's "Doubleness"

Hughes's efforts to create a poetry that truly evoked the spirit of black America involved a resolution of conflicts centering around the problem of identity. For Hughes, like W.E.B. Du

Bois, saw the black man's situation in America as a question of dual consciousness. As Du Bois wrote in his *The Souls of Black Folk* (1903): "It is a peculiar sensation, this double-consciousness, this sense of always looking at oneself through the eyes of others, of measuring one's soul by the tape of a world that looks on in amused contempt and pity. One ever feels his twoness—an American, a Negro; two souls, two thoughts, two unreconciled strivings; two warring ideals in one body, whose dogged strength alone keeps it from being torn asunder." Hughes was to speak of this same dilemma in his famous essay, published in 1926, concerning the problems of the black writer in America, "The Negro Artist and the Racial Mountain": "But this is the mountain standing in the way of any true Negro art in America—this urge within the race toward whiteness, the desire to pour racial individuality into the mold of American standardization, and to be as little Negro and as much American as possible." In *The Weary Blues*, Hughes presented the problem of dual consciousness quite cleverly by placing two parenthetical statements of identity as the opening and closing poems, and titling them "Proem" and "Epilogue." Their opening lines suggest the polarities of consciousness between which the poet located his own persona: "I Am a Negro" and "I, Too, Sing America." Within each of these poems, Hughes suggests the interrelatedness of the two identities: the line "I am a Negro" is echoed as "I am the darker brother" in the closing poem. Between the American and the Negro, a third identity is suggested: that of the poet or "singer." It is this latter persona which Hughes had assumed for himself in his attempt to resolve the dilemma of divided consciousness. Thus, within the confines of these two poems revolving around identity, Hughes is presenting his poetry as a kind of salvation. If one looks more closely at Hughes's organization of poems in the book, one finds that his true opening and closing poems are concerned not with identity but with patterns of cyclical time. "The Weary Blues" (the first poem) is about a black piano man who plays deep into the night until at last he falls into sleep "like a rock or a man that's dead." The last poem, on the other hand, suggests a rebirth, an awakening, after the long night of weary blues: "We have tomorrow / Bright before us / Like a flame." This pattern of cyclical time was adopted in the opening and closing poems of *Fine Clothes to the Jew*, which begins in sunset and ends in sunrise. Again, it is the blues singer (or poet) who recites the song: "Sun's a risin', / This is gonna be ma song." The poet's song, then, is Hughes's resolution to the problem of double consciousness, of being an American and being black. . . .

The Affirmation of Blackness

In Hughes's poetry, the central element of importance is the affirmation of blackness. Everything that distinguished Hughes's poetry from the white avant-garde poets of the twenties revolved around this important affirmation. Musical idioms, jazz rhythms, Hughes's special brand of "black-white" irony, and dialect were all dependent on the priority of black selfhood:

> I am a Negro
>
> Black as the night is black
>
> Black like the depths of my Africa.

Like Walt Whitman, Hughes began his career as a poet confident of his power. Unlike Whitman, however, who celebrated particular self . . . , Hughes celebrated racial, rather than individual, self. Hughes tended to suppress the personal element in his poetry, appropriating the first person singular as the fitting epitome of universal human tendencies embodied in race. "The Negro Speaks of Rivers" seems almost mystical in comparison to Whitman's physicality:

I've known rivers:

Ancient, dusky rivers.

My soul has grown deep like the rivers. . . .

Poetry as a Social Statement

Hughes was hesitant to introduce the element of the personal into his poetry. In an essay published in the journal *Phylon* in 1947 on his "adventures" as a social poet, Hughes remarked that his "earliest poems were social poems in that they were about people's problems—whole groups of people's problems—rather than my own personal difficulties.". . .

Perhaps the closest Hughes ever came to incorporating his personal anxiety into a poem was his "As I Grew Older," published initially in 1925, and later included in *The Weary Blues*. The poem is almost reduced to abstractions; it is a landscape of nightmare, a bleak and existential examination of blackness. The poet begins by recalling his "dream," once "bright like a sun," but now only a memory. A wall which separates the poet from his dream suddenly appears, causing him severe anxiety. It is at this point that the poet is thrust back upon himself and forced to seek an explanation for his dilemma:

Shadow.

I am black.

These two lines appearing at the center of the poem provide the key to his despair and to his salvation. As he begins to realize that his blackness is the cause of his being separated from his dream, he simultaneously realizes that blackness is central to his ontology. It is as much a physical reality as it is a metaphysical state of mind. In order for the dream to be restored, the spiritual and the physical blackness must be reintegrated. As the poet examines his hands, which are black, he discovers the source of his regeneration as a full person:

> My hands!
>
> My dark hands!
>
> Break through the wall!
>
> Find my dream!
>
> Help me to shatter this darkness,
>
> To smash this night,
>
> To break this shadow
>
> Into a thousand lights of sun,
>
> Into a thousand whirling dreams
>
> Of sun!

In order for the poet to transcend his temporal despair, he must accept the condition of his blackness completely and unequivocally. The poem thus ends, not in despair, but rather in a quest for self-liberation, dependent on the affirmation "I am black!" . . .

The Burden of Racial Complexity

The tension between his awareness of growing up black and his acceptance of the "dream" of America, however tenuously defined, provided the dynamic for his poetry. From an early age, Hughes developed the distinction between the social versus the physical implications of black identity in America: "You see, unfortunately, I am not black. There are lots of different kinds of blood in our family. But here in the United States, the word 'Negro' is used to mean anyone who has *any* Negro blood at all in his veins. In Africa, the word is more pure. It means *all* Negro, therefore *black*." During a trip to Africa as a merchant seaman in 1922, he discovered that the Africans who "looked at me . . . would not believe I was a Negro." The semantic confusion was of American origin. Whatever the semantic distinctions, Hughes desired to be accepted as Negro by the Africans, and was disappointed with their reaction to him....

Contradictions Within Racial and National Boundaries

Up until the time of his Southern lecture tour of 1931, his acquaintance with Southern mores had been merely peripheral. Indeed, he often began these programs by explaining how truly "American" his upbringing had been: "I began my programs by telling where I was born in Missouri, that I grew up in Kansas in the geographical heart of the country, and was, therefore very American." His audiences, which consisted largely of Southern Negroes, must have found his initial declaration of Americanism rather disorienting. As Hughes himself explained in his autobiography, this firsthand encounter with racial prejudice in the South provided an introduction to an important aspect of racial heritage to which he had never been fully exposed: "I found a great social and cultural gulf between the races in the South, astonishing to one who, like myself, from the North, had never known such uncompromising prejudices."

In a poem published in the *Crisis* in 1922, Hughes outlined his ambivalence toward the region in rather chilling imagery:

> The child-minded South
>
> Scratching in the dead fire's ashes
>
> For a Negro's bones.

He indicated in the poem's conclusion that the South had a strong attraction, but that he was more comfortable in resisting its allure:

> And I, who am black, would love her
>
> But she spits in my face

And I, who am black,

Would give her many rare gifts

But she turns her back upon me....

If Hughes feared the direct Southern confrontation during the twenties, he found much to admire in those Southern blacks who came to settle in the teeming cities of the North, and from them he derived material for his poetry. In seeking communal identity through them, Hughes overemphasized the exotic, as this passage from *The Big Sea* indicates: "I never tired of hearing them talk, listening to the thunder-claps of their laughter, to their troubles, to their discussions of the war and the men who had gone to Europe from the Jim Crow South.... They seemed to me like the gayest and the bravest people possible—these Negroes from the Southern ghettoes—facing tremendous odds, working and laughing and trying to get somewhere in the world." The passage suggests the attitude of a sympathetic observer rather than that of an engaged participant. In some ways, Hughes's attitude toward Southern Negroes was directly counter to that of his father's. According to Langston, the elder Hughes "hated Negroes. I think he hated himself, too, for being a Negro. He disliked all of his family because they were Negroes and remained in the United States." Hughes, on the other hand, proudly affirmed his racial heritage. Where his father rejected both race and country, Hughes could reject neither....

Hughes's Subject Is Always Race

Hughes's early attempts in the twenties to fill the role of poet laureate of the Negro led him to create a body of work that was organic in nature. The traditional literary sources of inspiration were for the most part bypassed. The source of his poetry was to be found in the anonymous, unheard black masses: their rhythms, their dialect, their lifestyles. Hughes sought to incorporate this untapped resource of black folk language into a new kind of poetry. His personal experiences, as related in his autobiography, combined with this folk material to provide thematic dimension to his work. The basic themes regarding the American dream and its possibilities for the black man were always present in his poetry. The tension between the unrealized dream and the realities of the black experience in America provided the dynamic. This tension between material and theme laid the groundwork for the irony which characterized Hughes's work at its best.

The Politics of Hughes's Lynching Poems

W. Jason Miller

W. Jason Miller is a professor at North Carolina State University. His book on lynching has received much academic attention, and he has contributed entries on blues and gospel music to The New Anthology of American Poetry: Vol. III, Postmodernisms 1950–Present.

During the 1950s Hughes's writings had branded him as a dangerous person. He was repeatedly accused of treason, and his work was often censored. To speak the truth, he had to walk a tight rope, refusing to ignore the subject of lynching that occurred even into the 1950s, and at the same time, present his subject in a manner that would enable publication and be taken seriously. Still, many readers saw his lynching poems as proof of treason. Often he was able to correct biased newspaper accounts of contemporary lynchings under the guise of merely telling a story rather than presenting a plea for reform. Another way he was able to write about lynching was to put the practice into historical context, to write of the past that still echoed in the present. The "Red Scare" of the 1950s led his publisher to exclude certain images and lines from Hughes's poems on racial injustice.

Because the cultural climate surrounding him in the 1950s consisted of blatant censorship and repeated accusations of communism, [Langston] Hughes's poetry deserves to be read within a framework in which he had to show discretion when speaking about lynching. Hughes discovered strategies

W. Jason Miller, "Poetry as Counternarrative: Retelling History," *Langston Hughes and American Lynching Culture*, 2011, pp. 116–119, 122–124. Copyright © 2011 by the University Press of Florida. Reprinted with permission of The University Press of Florida.

to address the topic of lynching in his poetry without being censored. He sometimes passed his poetry by "articulating other voices with such force and clarity that readers have assumed his complete disappearance from the poem." How and where Hughes passed poems about lynching is a subject that deserves to be revisited. . . .

Representatives of the dominant culture were unwilling to let a man whom they considered to be, at the very least, a Communist sympathizer berate America for its lynchings of African Americans. Unable to simply examine their own hypocrisy regarding the nation's professed core principles of freedom and justice, they incorrectly suspected that such critical attacks veiled deeper anti-American political purposes. They feared that his rhetoric was part of a larger underground movement called communism, which appeared to be bent on either undermining the structure of the established U.S. government or overthrowing the country. . . .

Hughes learned where and how he would and would not be allowed to pass on a personal level, and his poetry displays this same awareness. His negotiation of this constraint reveals that Hughes could simultaneously veil and document American lynching culture. Hughes's poetic designs that passed despite the constraints of censorship and red baiting reveal that he was unwilling to void this all-too-important subject from his writings. A reevaluation of his poetic works recovers his inventiveness, ambition, and determination in the face of these strict parameters.

Using Diplomacy to Correct Newspaper Accounts

This [viewpoint] explores Hughes's ability to successfully negotiate censorship so that he could still address the subject of lynching in his poetry. Hughes's references to lynching pass as he discusses the subject under the guise of simply retelling history. Hughes's poem "The Negro" is the central example of this strategy. In addition to retelling history, Hughes's work serves as a counternarrative to published news accounts of lynchings that appeared in the press. Hughes's poems, which appear to be only retelling history, first passed because they were presented in the guise of revisiting past events. They didn't read like rhetorical pleas for social change. Thus, they passed because they appear to concern issues that are distant and resolved rather than temporally close and in need of redress. Hughes's poetic counternarratives stand out because of their surprising complexity. "Mississippi" [was] one of Hughes's most important achievements in regard to writing counternarratives. In this poem, Hughes braids together allusions and autocitation as he rides new social currents that allow him to continue to extend and explore innovative ways of deepening our understanding of lynching.

Putting a Current Problem into Historical Context

Hughes invoked a deceptively simple strategy for passing his poems about American lynching culture on to the general public in the 1950s. This strategy included the "quasi-(in)visible dissent" practiced in the "rewriting" of "specific historical or cultural events." By appearing to be only retelling past history, his creative works read like narrative accounts focused on recovering cultural memories rather than angry protests pushing for immediate social or legislative change.

It is important to retrace when Hughes started this strategy of retelling history. He began applying the practice of retelling history around the same time he was drafting ideas for *Montage [of a Dream Deferred]* in the late 1940s. In fact, he first passed several of his lynching poems into his collection *One-Way Ticket* (1949); yet the high point of this practice came ten years later with "The Negro." Thinking back to an earlier image of Hughes testifying before [the Senate Permanent Subcommittee on Investigations] in 1953 reminds us of a startling irony. Had the committee decided to look in the very books placed on the table before Hughes, they would not have had to look far for a critique of American racism. Several of Hughes's poems that portrayed lynching under the guise of retelling history sat right before them under the cover of *One-Way Ticket*. The title poem of the collection that had been published only four years before this interrogation makes it clear why the speaker leaves the South by train and heads for the North. Near the end of the third stanza of the poem, he states he is tired of lynch mobs. Hughes also offered his readers four "silhouettes" of lynching in this collection. In "Blue Bayou," he continues the association between sunsets and lynching culture that first appeared in "The Negro Speaks of Rivers"; furthermore, the poem continues the dialogic and multivoiced narrative structure of "Christ in Alabama" as the mob, oppressed black lynch victim, and speaker in the poem each take turns speaking. "Silhouette," the third poem in the cycle, reads the lynched victim's body as a sign to the world of how white women are protected from black rapists. Hughes's poetry serves as the immortal site for which youth will never wither away as "Lynching Song" suggests that the lynched body refuses to die....

Using History to Protest Present Wrongs

Furthermore, his resentment is measurable as he portrays the eras of Rome, colonial America, and the Congo as mere precursors to the oppressions experienced in contemporary Mississippi. The present moment captured in the earliest word "now" and reiterated in the revised "still" is so easy to overlook that it gets ignored by many readers. Again, it is similar to what happens in approaches to "The Negro Speaks of Rivers." Both poems have earned a reputation for having captured the history of black citizens at the expense of examining their contemporary contexts. Just as the Nile River and the pyramids overshadow Hughes's own passage across the Missis-

Race in the Poetry of Langston Hughes

Emmett Till was a black 14-year-old Chicago boy who was kidnapped, tortured, and murdered for allegedly flirting with a white woman while he was visiting relatives in Mississippi. His body was weighted down and thrown into the Tallahatchie River. His brutal killing was a pivotal event leading to the civil rights movement in the United States. © AP Photo.

sippi River in "The Negro Speaks of Rivers," here the presence of Africa and the Congo work to veil the culminating statement of continued oppression and violence in America.

In regard to Hughes himself, we might imagine him venting his anger against the constraints of censorship, which have relegated his statements against lynching to the space of a mere single-line revision of one of his poems. In revisiting this deft revision, we feel the force and inertia this diminutive statement unleashes on 1950s American lynching culture. Moreover, the earlier publication date of 1922 creates the illusion that Hughes has merely included one of his older poems in his *Selected Poems*. This makes his revision nearly impossible to locate as a comment on a contemporary social horror. Hence, it passed.

This poem not only passed republication in *Selected Poems*, but Hughes also read it out loud in Washington, D.C., in October 1962. After being greeted at the White House by Mrs. Kennedy, Hughes joined almost three dozen other poets for the first national poetry festival. Hughes placed special emphasis on the original publication date of this poem during his formal poetry reading, as he quipped that the poem was the opening poem of his first ever book. Again, he was suggesting to his listeners that it was an old poem that offered no new critique of American racial violence. However, this single-line revision took on added significance as his opening poem at the festival was "Still Here," a poem in which Hughes's speaker announces that despite the fact that he's been "scared and battered," he remains defiantly "still here!"

The poem's ability to pass as a retelling of history reveals a great deal about its readers. Of most concern is the possibility that a reader in the late 1950s would perhaps acknowledge such lynchings as inevitable social practice; worse, twenty-first-century readers are sometimes so completely unaware of the practice of lynching that they simply ignore the line altogether. At all levels, many of our educational institutions have made contemporary readers more knowledgeable about George Washington and Julius Caesar than they have about the lynchings of Jesse Washington [an Africa American teenager burned and lynched in Waco, Texas, after being accused of raping and murdering a white woman] and Emmett Till [a fourteen-year-old African American boy who was brutally murdered after talking to a white woman].

Selected Poems contains three other poems that address lynching under the guise of documenting old history. "Blue Bayou," "Silhouette," and "Song for a Dark Girl" appear in the collection. Given the progression of this sequence in the collection, these three poems make their way into the collection as if they describe a past reality. They are located as motivations for leaving the South. This movement is completed by the three poems that follow them. In "The South," the speaker concludes that he will now go north, and the next poem, "Bound No'th Blues," documents his journey. "One-Way Ticket" continues this movement. Like many of Hughes's other works, this poem "promotes displacement" as an empowering experience.

These poems make it appear that such atrocities are a thing of the past that motivated blacks to engage in the inmigration to northern locals such as Chicago and Harlem. In short, it is only the single-line revision in "Negro" that reminds readers that lynching is a contemporary issue in need of social redress. It is not likely that Hughes suddenly felt lynching had gone away and was now a thing of the past. If he had, he would not have taken the time to revise the line in "Negro" or ensure that this poem was part of his high-profile program in Washington, D.C. It was not so much a necessary updating of an outdated poem as it was his choice to find an opening through which his disdain for lynching could be expressed.

Red Baiting and Censorship of Hughes

Extending Hughes's own use of analogy ..., why might we consider reading *The Langston Hughes Reader* (1958) and *Selected Poems of Langston Hughes* (1959) as lynched texts? Given the cultural climate in which they were published, neither includes any of Hughes's long attacks against American lynching culture. Among others, "Christ in Alabama," "Mississippi," "Three Lynching Songs," and "The Bitter River" are nowhere to be found in either collection. Given the immediacy of what is perhaps the most documented lynching in American history only three years earlier, the lynching of Emmett Till, this absence is more likely explained by the repercussions Hughes had to avoid among publishers and readers rather than a choice to drop this issue from his campaign.

Even more interesting, Hughes's "Not for Publication" appeared in print in the international publication *Black Orpheus* in 1959 rather than in his *Selected Poems* or *The Langston Hughes Reader*. Published by the Ministry of Education in Ibadan, Nigeria, editors Ulli Beier and Janheinz Jahn called *Black Orpheus* "A Journal of African and Afro-American Literature." Hughes's interest in Africa dated back at least to his first trip there in 1923. This interest had been growing even more recently as he had read his poetry to the accompaniment of a Nigerian drummer in celebration of African Freedom Day at Carnegie Hall on April 15, 1959. One month later, "Not for Publication" appeared in the pages of *Black Orpheus*, where his five poems were prominently listed in the magazine's table of contents. It was an important change from Hughes's inclusion of the poem in the *Crisis*.

Rage, Repudiation, and Endurance: Langston Hughes's Radical Writings

Christopher C. DeSantis

Christopher C. DeSantis is professor and director of the Graduate School at Illinois State University, where he teaches African American studies. He is a prolific scholar who has edited many volumes, including Langston Hughes and the Chicago Defender.

Langston Hughes's most socially radical writing about race came after the Great Depression. According to DeSantis, these works now get little attention, though they have been especially pertinent from the 1990s to the early decades of the twenty-first century when racial tensions have increased. What Hughes wrote in the 1930s did not always target the white man only. In an article in 1934, Hughes accused the black elite, especially those leading colleges, of producing obsequious students to serve white capitalism. The essay was a turning point when Hughes became less focused on folkways and more on social causes. He accused Negro leaders of catering too much to philanthropists and not paying sufficient attention to provoking social change. He also became less hopeful that change would occur, more critical of religion, and more attracted to radical political thinkers.

In *The Big Sea* Langston Hughes laments the close of the 1920s and the first years of the 1930s as the end of the period known as the Harlem Renaissance, a cultural movement of international significance which generated an outpouring

---

Christopher C. DeSantis, "Rage, Repudiation, and Endurance: Langston Hughes's Radical Writings," *The Langston Hughes Review*, vol. 12, no. 1, Spring 1993, pp. 31, 34–39. Copyright © 1993 by the Langston Hughes Society. All rights reserved. Reproduced by permission.

of African American art, literature, and criticism. The final chapters of Hughes's autobiography strike a tone of sadness, markedly different from the lively prose describing the writer's early years in vibrant Harlem. Hughes writes: "The generous 1920s were over. And my twenties almost over. I had four hundred dollars and a gold medal" (334–335). It is fitting that Hughes chose to mention his financial status in closing. With the Depression looming darkly over America, the hands of patrons who sustained many artists during the Harlem Renaissance were withdrawn. The prizes offered to promising writers by African American journals were fewer, and the stipends for submissions were of lesser amounts. Nevertheless, armed with the four hundred dollars that came with the 1931 Harmon Award ("Four hundred dollars! I had never had a job that paid more than twenty-two dollars a week."), Hughes scoffed at the national economic crisis: ". . . I'd finally and definitely made up my mind to continue being a writer—and to become a professional writer, making my living from writing" (335).

While Hughes was able to adhere to his goal of writing for a living, writing was certainly not the most pressing thing on his mind. The end of the Harlem Renaissance saw an increase in racial violence and economic hardship for the black masses in America. The beatings, lynchings, and daily humiliation of segregation which African Americans suffered in the South and elsewhere outraged Hughes. As a member of the African American community, Hughes accepted the responsibility to speak out against these injustices in his writing and to fight them in his daily life, at whatever cost to his own personal welfare. The body of writing which resulted from these turbulent years contains the most searing, ironic, and powerful poetry and prose that Hughes ever wrote. Often overlooked by readers and critics, Hughes's radical writings assume great significance when viewed in the context of the ever-increasing racial tensions we are witnessing in the 1990s. It is my intent here to reintroduce some of these works to readers and critics, lest we forget the powerful and far-reaching significance of Langston Hughes's famous question, "What happens to a dream deferred?"

The Scottsboro incident of 1931 set the tone for much of Hughes's radical poetry and prose that would emerge in the following years. The incident involved nine African American teenagers who were jailed in Scottsboro, Alabama, for allegedly raping two white prostitutes in an open railroad freight car. After a trial in Scottsboro, eight of the youths were sentenced to the electric chair and the ninth to life imprisonment. In *I Wonder as I Wander* Hughes reveals that Ruby Bates, one of the white women involved in the incident, later recanted her rape testimony and admitted that she fabricated the entire story (62). Arnold Rampersad notes in his biography of Hughes that whereas the NAACP hesitated to react to the indictment against the Scottsboro youths, "the International Labor Defense, the legal defense arm of the Communist Party, threw its energies into appealing the case and mobilizing public support for the defendants" (1,216). Taking the Scottsboro incident very much to heart, Hughes embraced the Communist Party as the only entity which seemed able, or at least willing, to help the nine youths. Though Hughes never formally joined the Communist Party, Rampersad found evidence to suggest that he served as honorary president of the League of Struggle for Negro Rights, an organization formed by the Communist Party to "bring the race problem into sharper relief" (1,217).

While Hughes was physically active lecturing and fundraising on behalf of the youths involved in the Scottsboro case, he also took a firm stand on the incident in his writing. Two searing essays responded to the call of the nine teenagers imprisoned in the state penitentiary at Kilby, Alabama. The first, "Southern Gentlemen, White Prostitutes, Mill-Owners, and Negroes," strikes a tone of disgust and defiance as Hughes poses a challenge to the African American community at large and specifically to the black leaders of the NAACP involved with the incident:

> But back to the dark millions—black and half-black, brown and yellow, with a gang of white fore-parents—like me. If these twelve million Negro Americans don't raise such a howl that the doors of Kilby Prison shake until the 9 youngsters come out ..., then let Dixie justice (blind and syphilitic as it may be) take its course, and let Alabama's Southern gentlemen amuse themselves burning 9 black boys till they're dead in the State's electric chair. (*Good Morning Revolution* 49)

Hughes ends the essay in mock prayer, signifying the bitter irony of the Scottsboro case in particular and the hypocritical structures of the Southern white social order in general: "Dear Lord, I never knew until now that white ladies (the same color as Southern gentlemen) traveled in freight trains ... Did you, world? ... And who ever heard of raping a prostitute?" (49)

Hughes's second essay on the Scottsboro incident, "Brown America in Jail: Kilby," was written after Hughes paid a visit to the Scottsboro youths while on a speaking tour through the South. Though eager to cheer the young men with some of his more humorous poems, Hughes notes in *I Wonder as I Wander* that the atmosphere in the prison had a feeling of desperation: "The youngest boy, Andy Wright, smiled. The others hardly moved their heads. The minister prayed, but none of the boys kneeled or even changed positions for his prayer. No heads bowed" (62). The essay is marked throughout by a tone of profound sadness and bitterness. Although one of the women involved in the Scottsboro incident recanted her rape testimony under oath, the youths remained in the "death house" of the prison. Where Hughes's first Scottsboro essay struck a tone of defiance and projected hope for

Race in the Poetry of Langston Hughes

justice, the second essay conveys the seeming futility of challenging a brutal and apparently hopeless racial situation in Alabama:

> For a moment the fear came: even for me, a Sunday morning visitor, the doors might never open again. WHITE guards held the keys. (The judge's chair protected like Pilate's.) And I'm only a nigger. Nigger. Nigger. Hundreds of niggers in Kilby Prison. Black, brown, yellow, near-white niggers. The guards, WHITE. Me—a visiting nigger. (*Good Morning Revolution* 50)

Although the tone of the essay is decidedly desperate, Hughes recognizes the Communist Party and a number of revolutionary writers for their interest in helping to change the racial situation in America. Through sarcasm Hughes drives the point home, further strengthening his ties with people and organizations which would prove to shape the nature of his writings in the years preceding the McCarthy hearings:

> (Keep silent, world. The State of Alabama washes its hands.) Eight brown boys condemned to death. No proven crime! Farce of a trial. Lies. Laughter. Mob. Music. Eight poor niggers make a country holiday. (Keep silent, Germany, Russia, France, young China, Gorki, Thomas Mann, Romain Rolland, Theodore Dreiser. Pilate washes his hands. Listen Communists, don't send any more telegrams to the Supreme Court. What's the matter? What's all this excitement about, over eight young niggers? Let the law wash its hands in peace.) (50)

Although at the time of the Scottsboro incident Hughes had achieved a certain degree of fame and was traveling around the country on a successful speaking tour, he realized that celebrity status was no protection against the bloody wrath of racial discrimination. A decade after the Scottsboro case, this proved equally true. "Roland Hayes Beaten (Georgia: 1942)," was written after the world-famous singer walked into a shoe store in Georgia, his home state, and was brutally beaten by a white store clerk. The beating occurred in 1942, during a war which was supposedly being fought to rid the world of racial supremacy, and in which many black soldiers saw active duty. In the poem Hughes addresses the theme of African Americans rising up against the oppression of whites, a theme that would become prevalent in much of his post-Scottsboro writings. He does not focus on the details of Hayes's bloody beating here. The power of the poem lies in the juxtaposition of humanity and nature. The comparison plays off in the stereotypical meek, humble, and accommodating nature of African Americans:

Negroes,

Sweet and docile,

Meek, humble, and kind:

Beware the day

They change their minds!

Wind

In the cotton fields,

Gentle breeze:

Beware the hour

It uproots trees!

—(*Select Poems* 167)

In the poem Hughes alludes to the dispossessed slaves in the Southern fields (the wind; transient and dynamic) and to the plantation overseers (the trees; established and static). Through this analogy Hughes suggests that the same oppression and brutality which resulted in slave revolts exists still, and will be dealt with in a similar manner. Fury will not sprout from the meek and humble, but rather from the oppressed, the brutalized and the displaced. Hughes's message is clear, and the clarity gains passion and fury when we consider the other radical writings—often overlooked by readers and critics—written during his distinguished career.

Race in the Poetry of Langston Hughes

In a scathing essay addressed to the leaders and educators of African American colleges throughout the nation, Hughes asserted that white people could no longer be blamed exclusively for the propagation of Jim Crow ethics and practices. "Cowards from the Colleges," first published in the *Crisis* in 1934, marked a turning point in Hughes's writing. Though he still concerned himself with documenting folk mannerisms, patterns of speech, and ways of life of common black people, Hughes perceived in the educated black elite an invidious pattern of behavior that seemed to encourage rather than ameliorate the social codes that served to keep the African American community in the margins of American society: "To combine these charges very simply: Many of our institutions apparently are not trying to make men and women of their students at all—they are doing their best to produce spineless Uncle Toms, uninformed and full of mental and moral evasions" (*Good Morning Revolution* 57). In backing up his assertions, Hughes cites two incidents in which blatant racism was glossed over by college administrators worried about the possible danger of offending white patrons of the college. The first incident concerned Juliette Derricotte, the dean of women at Fisk University, who died after an automobile accident because she was refused treatment by white Georgia hospitals (Rampersad, 1,223). The second incident involved the football coach of Alabama's A&M Institute at Normal, who was beaten to death by a mob in Birmingham while attempting to see his team play (Rampersad, 1,223). Outraged by the two incidents which occurred during the same weekend, students at Hampton, where Hughes was lecturing at the time, attempted to band together and protest the racial violence. Citing the school's policy of "moving slowly and quietly, and with dignity," Major Brown, the dean of men at Hampton, and an African American, effectively killed the protest. Hughes writes:

> On and on he talked. When he had finished, the students knew quite clearly that they could not go ahead with their

protest meeting. (The faculty had put up its wall.) They knew they would face expulsion and loss of credits if they did so. The result was that the Hampton students held no meeting of protest over the mob-death of their own alumnus, nor the death on the road ... of one of the race's finest young women. The brave and manly spirit of that little group ... was crushed by the official voice of Hampton speaking through its Negro Major Brown. (*Good Morning Revolution* 59)

Hughes's anger at some of the black leaders and institutions of higher learning did not, of course, go unexpressed in his poetry. Although some of the intellectuals in Harlem during the Renaissance found books such as *The Weary Blues* and *Fine Clothes to the Jew* disturbing because of their glamorization of the black working class, those texts did not offend nearly so much as the more radical verse Hughes wrote in the 1930s. "To Certain Negro Leaders," a poem first published in *New Masses*, addresses in sparse and angry language the bitter frustrations Hughes attempted to document in "Cowards from the Colleges":

Voices crying the wilderness,

At so much per word

From the white folks:

"Be meek and humble,

All you niggers,

And do not cry

Too loud."

—(*Good Morning Revolution*, 14)

Hughes cryptically posits here the dangerous ramifications white patronage and philanthropy pose to African American institutions. Money becomes a shackle to the receiving institutions; the maker of the gift holds the power to tighten it at will. Hughes arrived at these conclusions through his bitter experiences with Charlotte Mason during the Harlem Renais-

Race in the Poetry of Langston Hughes

On March 26, 1953, Langston Hughes spoke before the Senate Permanent Subcommittee on Investigations in Washington, DC. Hughes testified before the subcommittee that he formerly had been sympathetic to the Soviet form of government but that he had never been a member of the Communist Party. © AP Photo.

sance. When Hughes expressed a desire to try different things with his poetry, Mason's patronage was quickly, and finally, withdrawn.[1]

The hypocrisy which seemed to fester behind philanthropic fronts troubled Hughes long after the end of the Harlem Renaissance and the largesse of wealthy patrons who supported it. Addressing the first American Writers' Congress in 1935, Hughes called on African American writers to expose these hypocrisies through their novels, stories, poems, and articles:

> The lovely grinning face of Philanthropy—which gives a million dollars to a Jim Crow school, but not one job to a graduate of that school; which builds a Negro hospital with second-rate equipment, then commands black patients and student-doctors to go there whether they will or no; or

which, out of the kindness of its heart, erects yet another separate, segregated, shut-off, Jim Crow Y.M.C.A. (*Good Morning Revolution* 125)

Hughes believed in the transformative powers of the written word, and cautioned writers about using their art for purposes other than social change. This rhetoric, of course, was first espoused by Hughes during the Harlem Renaissance. In "The Negro Artist and the Racial Mountain," published in 1926, Hughes called for the formation of a "racial art" which would lead to the creation of a distinct black aesthetic. He denounced writers who believed their art came first, their race second. More significant here, Hughes believed in a social force inherent in art, and considered it a basic duty of black artists to channel this force toward social change. At his speech before the first American Writers' Congress in 1935,[2] Hughes called on black writers to fulfill this basic duty:

> Sure, the moon still shines over Harlem. Shines over Scottsboro. Shines over Birmingham, too, I reckon. Shines over Cordie Cheek's grave, down South. Write about the moon if you want to. Go ahead. This is a free country. But there are certain very practical things American Negro writers can do. And must do. There's a song that says, "the time ain't long." That song is right. Something has to change in America—and change soon. We must help that change to come. The moon's still shining as poetically as ever, but all the stars on the flag are dull. (And the stripes, too). (*Good Morning Revolution* 126)

Hughes's poems of this period, while adhering to the basic artistic ideals established in the 1920s, were far removed from the optimism generated by the artists of the Harlem Renaissance. With the Depression came more hunger, more oppression, and more racial violence. These facets of American life were certainly not new to Hughes, but there seemed during this period to be something more evil and more dangerous with which African Americans had to contend. Not content to see the African American community merely endure, Hughes felt that revolution was a necessary end:

> I am so tired of waiting,
>
> Aren't you,
>
> For the world to become good
>
> And beautiful and kind?
>
> Let us take a knife
>
> And cut the world in two—
>
> And see what worms are eating
>
> At the rind.
>
> —(*Good Morning Revolution* 36)

With Hughes's disgust at the generally bleak state of life in America came a profound mistrust of religion, particularly directed at those people who used Christianity as a cloak behind which to hide their oppressive actions. "Goodbye Christ" most explicitly conveys Hughes's attitude at the time. Where the call for revolution was softened by imagery in "Tired," here Hughes unleashes words of anger and bitterness which make clear his political posture:

> Listen, Christ,
>
> You did alright in your day, I reckon—
>
> But that day's gone now.
>
> They ghosted you up a swell story, too,
>
> Called it Bible—
>
> But it's dead now.
>
> The popes and the preachers've
>
> Made too much money from it.
>
> They've sold you to too many.
>
> —(*Good Morning Revolution* 36–37)

In the poem Hughes examines, or rather obliterates, the tenets set forth in a supposedly Christian country. If a majority of Americans do indeed call themselves Christians, why then do we witness so much suffering, so much oppression? During the time in which the poem was written, Hughes made a journey to the Soviet Union and saw socialism working, whereas in America, Christianity had failed.[3] Though resources in the Soviet Union were meager, Hughes notes the fact that "white and black, Asiatic and European, Jew and Gentile stood alike as citizens on an equal footing protected from racial inequalities by the law" (*Good Morning Revolution* 133). Hughes thus called for a rethinking of dominant American beliefs and an acceptance of the tenets of Marxism:

Goodbye,

Christ Jesus Lord God Jehovah,

Beat it on away from here now.

Make way for a new guy with no religion at all—

A real guy named

Marx Communist Lenin Peasant Stalin Worker ME. . . .

—(*Good Morning Revolution* 37)

The trip to the Soviet Union obviously had a profound effect on much of Hughes's writing during this period. A little more than a decade after the visit, Hughes wrote a series of articles addressing his experiences. These pieces appeared in Hughes's weekly "Here To Yonder" column in the *Chicago Defender*, an influential African American newspaper. Though the anger and bitterness evident in his 1930s writings lost intensity as Hughes moved into the 1940s, his vision of humanity remained unchanged. Indeed, the first article in the series deals mainly with the humanitarian aspects of the Soviet Union:

> There is one country in the world that has NO Jim Crow of any sort, NO UNEMPLOYMENT of any sort, NO PROSTI-

TUTION or demeaning of the human personality through poverty, NO LACK OF EDUCATIONAL FACILITIES for all of its young people, and NO LACK OF SICK CARE or dental care for everybody. That country is the Soviet Union. (*Good Morning Revolution* 80)

Hughes was not completely unrealistic or idealistic about the Soviet Union, and was quick to point out that it was not a paradise. He recognized the meagerness of resources to be a serious problem, but found the Soviet way of life and governance to be ultimately superior to that in America: "[The] steps toward an earthly paradise reach higher today on the soil of the Soviet Union than they do anywhere else in this troubled world. And the future of the Soviet Union is based on more concrete modern social achievements than that of any other existing state" (80). Hughes bases this assertion on many factors, one of the most important being the position of women in the Soviet Union. He was very much impressed that prostitution had been wiped out, linking the demeaning profession to capitalism and greed: "In many great cities of the capitalist world, I have seen poor girls of high school age selling their favors as cheaply as a pair of stockings... During the American depression, the streets of our big cities were full of such women. Poverty, the economic root of prostitution, is gone in the Soviet Union" (86). Where the general welfare of the people in the Soviet Union seemed superior to that in America, however, Hughes found that the Soviet people did not enjoy the freedom of speech which was largely taken for granted in the United States. Heads of government were assured of not being ridiculed publicly, for the price of denouncing a public official was often a rather stiff prison sentence. Hughes both lamented and praised the Soviet newspapers for not printing crime news or racially derogatory statements: "Nice juicy murders and big black brutes are both missing from their pages. Soviet headlines are not as exciting in a sensational way as ours" (91).

Despite its faults, however, Hughes saw in the Soviet Union a degree of hope which seemed sadly absent in America. While the African American community was still suffering the same violence and oppression it had endured for years, followers of the Soviet doctrines seemed infinitely better off. Hughes addresses this idea in "Lenin," one of his last poems to endorse communism:

Lenin walks around the world.

Frontiers cannot bar him.

Neither barracks nor barricades impede.

Nor does barbed wire scar him.

Lenin walks around the world.

Black, brown, and white receive him.

Language is no barrier.

The strangest tongues believe him.

Lenin walks around the world.

The sun sets like a scar.

Between the darkness and the dawn

There rises a red star.

—(*Good Morning Revolution* 94)

Although Hughes ultimately abandoned his support of communism shortly after "Lenin" was written, his love for the Soviet Union and its people remained. Arnold Rampersad has noted that Hughes's renunciation of communism did not result in a break with all organizations on the left, and that Hughes continued to support groups that fell under the scrutiny of Joseph McCarthy's investigations (2, 95). Retaining these ties, it seems, made Hughes amply suspect. On March 26, 1953, Hughes appeared before McCarthy's Senate Permanent Subcommittee on Investigations to explain and account for this "anti-American," radical past. At the hearing, Hughes offered a prepared statement which effectively repudiated his radical writings and saved him from serious charges by the committee. When asked by Roy Cohn, the head examiner, to describe the time period in which he sympathized with the Soviet form of government and when that period ended, Hughes replied:

> There was no abrupt ending, but I would say, that roughly the beginnings of my sympathies with Soviet ideology were coincident with the Scottsboro case, the American depression, and that they ran through for some 10 or 12 years or more, certainly up to the Nazi-Soviet Pact, and perhaps, in relation to some aspects of the Soviet ideology, further, because we were allies, as you know, with the Soviet Union during the war. So some aspects of my writing would reflect that relationship, that war relationship. (United States 74)

When further questioned by Cohn as to what exactly caused his change in ideology, Hughes offered an answer which amply satisfied the committee:

> The Nazi-Soviet Pact was, of course, very disillusioning ... and then further evidences of, shall we say, spreading imperialist aggression. My own observations in 1931–32, as a writer, which remained with me all the time, of the lack of freedom of expression in the Soviet Union for writers, which I never agreed with before I went there or afterward—those things gradually began to sink in deeper and deeper. And then, in our own country, there has been, within the last 10 years, certainly within the war period, a very great increase in the rate of acceleration of improvement in race relations. (United States 75)

In closing, Hughes was asked if he was in any way mistreated by the staff or the committee involved with the investigation. His reply could only have served to warm the hearts of the very people who had caused him much pain: "I must say that I was agreeably surprised at the courtesy and friendliness with which I was received. . . . [Senator Dirksen] was, I thought, most gracious and in a sense helpful in defining for me the area of this investigation; and the young men who had to interrogate me, of course, had to interrogate me" (United States 83).

Rampersad has demonstrated that by cooperating with McCarthy and the committee, Hughes was choosing the lesser of two evils: "He could defy the body and destroy much of his effectiveness in the black world. Or he could cooperate, draw the disapproval, even the contempt, of the white left, but keep more or less intact the special place he had painstakingly carved out within the black community" (2,219). Given Hughes's love for his community which he had held since he began writing, Rampersad suggested that the choice was perhaps easy to make. Although Hughes repudiated a body of writing that was so important to a turbulent period in his life, the choice allowed him to continue doing what he loved best. After the hearing he resumed the admirable task of making a living as a writer, perhaps subconsciously secure in the fact that his writings, including the ones he apparently repudiated, were tucked safely away in the archives of universities across the country.

Notes

1. The first volume of Rampersad's biography documents the relationship between Charlotte Mason and Langston Hughes during the Harlem Renaissance. For a fictional portrait of this relationship, see Langston Hughes, "The Blues I'm Playing," In *The Ways of White Folks* (1934; New York: Vintage 1971) 96–120.

2. The rhetoric and ideology of "To Negro Writers" are firmly grounded in Socialist discourse but still adhere to the ideals established during the Harlem Renaissance.

3. Hughes traveled to the Soviet Union in June 1932, with a group of twenty-two young African Americans to make *Black and White*, a motion picture commissioned

by the Meschrabpom Film Corporation. Although the film was not completed, Hughes remained in Russia for one year.

Works Cited

Hughes, Langston. *The Big Sea*. 1940. New York: Thunder's Mouth Press, 1989.

_____. *Good Morning Revolution: Uncollected Writings of Social Protest* by Langston Hughes. Ed. Faith Berry. New York: Lawrence Hill, 1973.

_____. *I Wonder as I Wander*. 2956. New York: Thunder's Mouth Press, 1988.

_____. "The Negro Artist and the Racial Mountain." *Nation* 122 (June 23, 1926): 692–694.

_____. *Selected Poems*. 1959. New York: Vintage, 1974.

Rampersad, Arnold. *The Life of Langston Hughes*. 2 vols. New York: Oxford UP, 1986, 1988.

United States. State Department Information Program. "Testimony of Langston Hughes, Accompanied by his Counsel, Frank D. Reeves." (March 26, 1953): 73–83.

Social Issues in Literature

CHAPTER 3

Contemporary Perspectives on Race

Laws in 2011 and 2012 Are Designed to Diminish Minority Votes

Wendy R. Weiser and Lawrence Norden

Wendy R. Weiser directs the Democracy Program at the Brennan Center for Justice at New York University School of Law. Lawrence Norden is deputy director of the Brennan Center's Democracy Program.

The Brennan Center for Justice reported on the changes in 2011 and 2012 voting laws and their effect on African American voters. The most obvious aim is not to broaden the franchise but to restrict it. The supporters of these laws claim that they are necessary to fight voter fraud, but statistics show that fraud is not a problem. The state of Florida has received the attention of many investigators who argue that the new laws there "disproportionately impact Florida's minority voters." For example, minority voting depends on voter registration drives that the state is seeking to stop. The poor rarely have passports. The required photo identification is difficult and costly to obtain. Getting to the Department of Motor Vehicles, standing in long lines there, and paying fees are obstacles to the poor and elderly in obtaining identification. Eliminating Sunday voting has also been a hardship because Sunday is a day when African American churches and other groups provide transportation to the polls.

Over the past century, our nation expanded the franchise and knocked down myriad barriers to full electoral participation. In 2011, however, that momentum abruptly shifted.

Wendy R. Weiser and Lawrence Norden, "Voting Law Changes in 2012," Brennan Center for Justice, New York University School of Law, 2011, pp. 1, 15, 21–24, 33. Copyright © 2011 by Brennan Center for Justice. All rights reserved. Reproduced by permission.

State governments across the country enacted an array of new laws making it harder to register or to vote. Some states require voters to show government-issued photo identification, often of a type that as many as one in ten voters do not have. Other states have cut back on early voting, a hugely popular innovation used by millions of Americans. Two states reversed earlier reforms and once again disenfranchised millions who have past criminal convictions but who are now taxpaying members of the community. Still others made it much more difficult for citizens to register to vote, a prerequisite for voting.

Restrictive Legislation Will Hinder Minority and Poor Voters

These new restrictions fall most heavily on young, minority, and low-income voters, as well as on voters with disabilities. This wave of changes may sharply tilt the political terrain for the 2012 election. Based on the Brennan Center's analysis of the 19 laws and two executive actions that passed in 14 states, it is clear that:

- These new laws could make it significantly harder for more than five million eligible voters to cast ballots in 2012.

- The states that have already cut back on voting rights will provide 171 electoral votes in 2012—63 percent of the 270 needed to win the presidency.

- Of the 12 likely battleground states, as assessed by an August [2011] *Los Angeles Times* analysis of Gallup polling, five have already cut back on voting rights (and may pass additional restrictive legislation), and two more are currently considering new restrictions.

States have changed their laws so rapidly that no single analysis has assessed the overall impact of such moves. Although it is too early to quantify how the changes will impact voter turnout, they will be a hindrance to many voters at a time when the United States continues to turn out less than two-thirds of its eligible citizens in presidential elections and less than half in midterm elections....

The Costs of Voter ID

The high cost of implementing voter ID [identification] laws was a big issue this session, when states were facing serious fiscal crises. States that pass voter ID laws must, according to court decisions, incur a range of costs, including the costs of providing free photo IDs to voters who do not have them, ensuring that IDs are reasonably accessible to all voters, and educating the public and election officials. Although there was widespread agreement that voter ID laws entail necessary costs, there were disputes over what those costs would be, with bill opponents accusing proponents of dramatically understating the costs.

The high cost of voter ID requirements caused local and county election officials in some states—including Iowa, Pennsylvania, and Wisconsin—to oppose new voter ID laws. They also deterred legislators in Nebraska and Iowa, two states that considered, but did not pass, voter ID legislation this year.

Nebraska. The fiscal note attached to Nebraska's photo ID bill (L.B. 239), estimated negligible costs associated with its implementation, assuming that only voters who could prove they were indigent would be provided with free IDs. Opponents argued that forcing voters to prove indigence before they could be provided with a photo ID could subject the bill to constitutional challenge, and argued that all IDs should be free. The original sponsor of the bill, Senator Charlie Janssen, proposed an amendment to the bill that would have added non-photo ID and voter registration confirmation cards to the list of acceptable forms of voting identification. This drew a rebuke from Larry Dix, director of the Nebraska Association of County Officials, who said the amendment would increase costs for the counties without providing any extra security. "I don't see that the [proposed amendment] solves the problem at all," he said, "there's no security in that." Ultimately, the bill failed to leave committee and therefore died when the legislative session ended.

Iowa. The Iowa State Association of County Auditors (ISACA)—a bipartisan organization representing county auditors, who are responsible for administering elections at the county level—opposed the voter ID bill proposed in their state. ISACA conducted an independent study of the impact of voter ID measures ... and found that the proposed Iowa bill would impose too high a cost and burden on local election jurisdictions to justify its adoption. As one county auditor put it, the legislation would be an "unfunded mandate" on counties, who would have to bear the brunt of meeting the obligation of "educating the public and the voter [about the bill's requirements]." As a result, the association voted to officially oppose H.F. 95. Both Democratic and Republican representatives in ISACA opposed the measure, with not one person voting to support it and with 16 of 60 county representatives choosing to remain neutral. According to Mike Gronstal, the Senate majority leader, the opposition from ISACA was one of the main reasons the bill ultimately failed....

No Rationale for Restrictive Laws

Bills placing new restrictions on voter registration groups have been proposed in at least seven states—California (passed in both houses; awaiting governor's action), Florida, Illinois (pending), Mississippi (failed), Nevada (restrictions removed by amendment), New Mexico (failed), North Carolina (pending), and Texas.

These bills have been signed into law in Florida and Texas. Florida and Texas stand out as two states that have long histories of restricting voter registration drives, and the new laws passed in this session will make both states further outliers in limiting this activity. Neither state had reported cases of registration fraud linked to voter registration drives in the past election cycle, nor any other apparent precipitating cause for the further regulations imposed by these bills. . . .

Florida has a history of implementing restrictive rules for voter registration drives—rules that have been successfully challenged before. (The Brennan Center for Justice has litigated twice in the past on behalf of Florida civic groups to challenge these restrictions.). . .

Florida's History of Voter Restriction and Discrimination

Between 2009 and 2011, there was no controversy in Florida involving voter registration and indeed nothing to suggest why the state legislature again took up the subject of restricting voter registration drives. Proponents of H.B. 1355, the omnibus voting bill that included new restrictions on voter registration drives, merely claimed that they sought to reduce fraud. They also made it very clear that they wanted to make voting harder. The bill's sponsor, Florida State Senator Mike Bennett (R-Bradenton), was quoted as saying "But I have to tell you, I don't have a problem making it harder. I want people in Florida to want to vote as bad as that person in Africa who walks 200 miles across the desert. This should not be easy. This should be something you should do with a passion." Florida State Senator Ellyn Bogdanoff agreed: "Democracy should not be a convenience," she said. . . .

The Florida law is currently being considered by a federal court for "preclearance," federal approval required for jurisdictions covered under section 5 of the Voting Rights Act because of a history of discrimination. Section 5 requires covered jurisdictions to supply evidence that changes to a state's election laws will not harm minority voters before those changes may go into effect. Five of Florida's sixty-seven counties are covered jurisdictions, where H.B. 1355 remains on hold awaiting preclearance; Secretary of State [Kurt S.] Browning has ordered election supervisors in the sixty-two non-covered counties to implement the law. Voting rights advocates have submitted evidence to both the Department of Justice and the federal court arguing that the new restrictions on voter registration drives, as well as the bill's other provisions reducing early voting days and eliminating cross-county address changes at the polls, will disproportionately impact Florida's minority voters.

The Impact of New Voting Laws on Minority Voters

Opponents of the bills and laws detailed in this report frequently point to their negative impact on the ability of African American and Latino citizens to vote, and with good reason: There is substantial evidence that these laws will make it far more difficult for minorities than whites to vote.

For instance, Florida's new law—which places so many new burdens on voter registration drive activity that most groups have discontinued their voter registration activities in the state—will almost certainly hit African American and Hispanic voters hardest. In Florida, U.S. Census Bureau data from the 2004 and 2008 election cycles show that both African Americans and Hispanics rely more heavily than white voters on community-based voter registration drives; in fact, African American and Hispanic citizens in Florida are more than twice as likely to register to vote through such drives as white voters.

Similarly, the most restrictive voter ID laws, which only allow a small number of specified government-issued photo IDs to vote, seem certain to create more burdens for minority citizens. According to one study, as many as 25% of African American voters do not possess a current and valid form of government-issued photo ID, compared to 11% of voters of all races. And the kinds of government-issued IDs that are permitted in the various state laws often put minorities at an even greater disadvantage. For instance, ... the new Texas voter ID law permits voters to use a concealed handgun license as proof of identity, but precludes voters from using a student ID, even if the student ID was issued by a state university. As the Texas Department of Public Safety recently noted, African Americans are significantly underrepresented among the state's handgun license holders. Of the more than 100,000 concealed handgun licenses issued in Texas last year, only 7.69% were issued to African Americans, even though African Americans constitute 12.1% of the state's voting-age population. In contrast, African Americans are more likely to attend a public university in Texas than whites. According to the 2009 American Community Survey, 8.0% of voting-age African Americans in Texas attended a public university compared with only 5.8% of voting-age whites.

New restrictions on early voting will also have their biggest impact on people of color. Opponents of these restrictions have been particularly angered by the efforts to eliminate Sunday early voting, which they see as explicitly targeting African American voters. Florida eliminated early voting on the last Sunday before Election Day, and Ohio has eliminated early voting on Sundays entirely. There is substantial statistical and anecdotal evidence that African Americans (and to a lesser extent Hispanics) vote on Sundays in proportionately far greater numbers than whites. For instance, in the 2008 general election in Florida, 33.2% of those who voted early on the last Sunday before Election Day were African American and 23.6% were Hispanic, whereas African Americans constituted just 22.7% of all early voters for all early voting days, and Hispanics just 11.6%. ...

Early Voting on Sunday and the Black Vote

Among the most controversial early voting reductions has been the partial or full eliminations of early voting on Sunday. Ohio has eliminated in-person early voting on Sundays entirely, Florida has eliminated it on the last Sunday before Election Day, and a North Carolina bill proposes to eliminate all in-person early voting on Sundays. Critics have cried foul, arguing that these measures are "aimed squarely at reducing African-American turnout." In particular, these critics charge, it is common for black voters to go to the polls in large groups on Sundays, after church, and for some African American churches to organize "Souls to the Polls" voting drives. In Florida, a local Democratic club leader noted that "churches had either hired buses, or used their buses to take people to the polls, or even suspending [sic] the service on the Sunday before." The *Palm Beach Post* stated that "[m]ore than half of the black voters in the [November 2008] election voted before Election Day and many of them went on [the] final Sunday." In Ohio, WilliAnn Moore, coordinator of the northwest Ohio district of the NAACP [National Association for the Advancement of Colored People], labeled Ohio's new legislation "voter-suppression legislation," taking specific aim at the part of the law that eliminated Sunday early voting, noting that it had become a regular practice in the black community for voters to "pile into vans after church to cast their ballots."

Where available, the evidence supports the contention that black (and to a lesser extent Hispanic) voters used Sunday early voting in numbers proportionally greater than other groups. For instance, in the 2008 general election in Florida, 33.2% of those who voted early on the last Sunday before Election Day were black and 23.6% were Hispanic, whereas blacks constituted 22.7% of all early voters statewide (for all early voting days) and Hispanics constituted 11.6%.

Among those who supported these laws, which reduced early voting in additional ways, there was little public explanation of why Sunday was specifically targeted, other than the general argument that the elimination was needed to reduce costs and administrative burden. In North Carolina, Senator Jim Davis, the sponsor of his state's bill, opined that "we were just trying to minimize the time early voting polls were open ... so the expense is not so great for local election boards ... [e]verybody who wants to vote still can vote." One of his colleagues, Senate Leader Phil Berger, got closer to the issue of eliminating Sunday voting stating, "It's my understanding that there are some folks who feel that Sundays should not be mixed politics and religion, that it's probably better to have a day that folks take a day off from politics. That's one of the comments that I've heard."

Defusing Implicit Bias

Jonathan Feingold and Karen Lorang

Jonathan Feingold and Karen Lorang, both graduates of the University of California Los Angeles (UCLA) School of Law, were editors of the issue of the UCLA Law Review Discourse *from which this viewpoint was taken.*

Explicit racism is different from implicit bias. Attention needs to be paid to the connection between the growing availability of guns and "implicit" racial bias. Studies now show that both black and white armed people are more likely to shoot unarmed black men than white men. The issue became ignited with the 2012 shooting of an unarmed black teenager, Trayvon Martin, by a white/Latino man, George Zimmerman. The failure of police to arrest Zimmerman initially was largely attributed to the racial attitude toward the victim. Police bias and gun laws need to be addressed. Target training for gun owners needs to be required, and police training in the role of implicit bias could possibly reduce the number of deaths. Another primary obstacle in reducing the shooting of unarmed black men is permissive self-defense or "stand your ground" laws, which discourage retreating from a confrontation and allow the use of force in self-defense.

The February 2012 killing of Trayvon Martin reignited the national conversation about race and violence. Despite the sheer volume of discussion and debate arising from this tragedy, insufficient attention has been paid to the potentially deadly mix of guns and implicit bias. Evidence of implicit bias and its power to alter real-world behavior is stronger now

---

Jonathan Feingold and Karen Lorang, "Defusing Implicit Bias," *UCLA Law Review Discourse*, vol. 59, 2012, pp. 212–219, 223–228. Copyright © 2012 by Jonathan Feingold and Karen Lorang. Reprinted with permission. All rights reserved. The notes from the original article have been removed.

than ever. A growing body of research on "shooter bias" reveals that, as a result of implicit bias, both white and black Americans are more likely to shoot unarmed black men than unarmed white men. While the science cannot tell us whether implicit bias caused George Zimmerman to shoot Trayvon Martin, this moment marks an opportunity to examine the connection between implicit bias and guns. Defusing implicit bias is a daunting task, but the stakes are too high to ignore the problem. States, responsible for laws regulating gun ownership and use, must help defuse implicit bias before it becomes deadly.

Trayvon Martin's Shooter

Seventeen-year-old Trayvon Martin was fatally shot while out walking on February 26, 2012. On the day he was killed, Trayvon and his father were visiting a friend in a gated community in Sanford, Florida. Trayvon walked to the local 7-Eleven, where he bought Skittles and an iced tea. George Zimmerman, a local neighborhood watch captain, was driving in his SUV when he noticed Trayvon walking back from the store. Unlike Zimmerman, Trayvon was black. Trayvon was wearing a hooded sweatshirt. Zimmerman called the police because he felt Trayvon looked "real suspicious." The police explicitly instructed Zimmerman not to follow Trayvon.

Exactly what happened next is the subject of much debate, and we make no attempt to resolve any factual disputes here. What is clear is that although Trayvon was unarmed, Zimmerman eventually left his car and shot and killed Trayvon with a 9mm handgun. After police arrived at the scene, "Zimmerman was taken into custody, questioned and released."

Zimmerman claimed from the outset that he acted in self-defense. According to Zimmerman's father, at some point during the encounter Zimmerman lost sight of Trayvon and began walking back to his car. Before reaching his car, Trayvon reappeared and allegedly punched Zimmerman "in the nose and slammed his head into the sidewalk." In the ensuing moments, Zimmerman pulled his pistol from his waistband and shot Trayvon in the chest.

Under a 2005 Florida statute, Zimmerman had no duty to retreat before using deadly force in self-defense as long as he was attacked in a place where he had a lawful right to be. Florida law states the following:

> A person who is not engaged in an unlawful activity and who is attacked in any other place where he or she has a right to be has no duty to retreat and has the right to stand his or her ground and meet force with force, including deadly force if he or she reasonably believes it is necessary to do so to prevent death or great bodily harm to himself or herself or another or to prevent the commission of a forcible felony.

In light of Zimmerman's self-defense claim, the Sanford police initially concluded they had insufficient evidence to arrest Zimmerman on a manslaughter charge.

Immediate Public Outrage at the Killing

Coverage of the case evolved slowly. A local television channel covered the killing the following day, and Florida newspapers picked up the story within a week. The national news media began reporting on the case in mid-March. As the story spread, the "reluctance to arrest Zimmerman sparked a national outcry, with many observers suspecting that Zimmerman, who is half-white and half-Latino, was given a break because of his race, and the race of the young man he fatally shot." The public response to the incident included numerous rallies and protests. Supporters, including the Miami Heat basketball team and a congressman on the House floor, symbolically wore hooded sweatshirts in solidarity.

Zimmerman's Arraignment

As the public response grew, Florida Governor Rick Scott appointed State Attorney Angela Corey to act as special prosecutor on the case. On April 11, the state charged Zimmerman with second-degree murder, and he turned himself in to authorities. On April 20, Zimmerman took the stand during his bail hearing and apologized to Trayvon's parents. Zimmerman was formally arraigned on May 8. Zimmerman did not attend the arraignment, but his attorney, Mark O'Mara, entered a written plea of not guilty and communicated Zimmerman's wish to waive his right to a speedy trial. As a result, Zimmerman's trial is not expected to begin before October 2012. A pretrial hearing has been set for August 8, 2012....

Unpacking the varied responses to Trayvon's death requires a close look at the growing body of scientific evidence concerning implicit bias. At a basic level, implicit bias refers to the subconscious associations we make between a particular object and the meanings we attach to it. In the context of human beings, implicit biases result in automatic associations between an individual's race and corresponding stereotypes and attitudes. Perhaps most importantly, we now know that implicit bias predicts actual behavior....

The Question of Racial Discrimination

Some, including Trayvon Martin's parents, have implied that Trayvon's death was the result of racial profiling or racial discrimination. Others, including Zimmerman's father and his first attorney, rejected suggestions that race played any role in Zimmerman's decision to pursue and ultimately to shoot Trayvon. Given the conflicting accounts and understandings of how events unfolded, how can we know whether race was a factor in Trayvon's death? What evidence would prove that race motivated Zimmerman? Was this a moment of racial profiling? Is it fair to call Zimmerman a racist?

These questions lie at the heart of the national conversation that developed around this tragedy. Before trying to answer these questions, it is crucial to clearly define the term "racial discrimination." The dominant conception of racial discrimination in the current debate has squarely reflected the

U.S. Supreme Court's antidiscrimination jurisprudence. Under the court's current approach, known as disparate treatment theory, racial discrimination exists if, and only if, an identifiable perpetrator treats a victim in a harmful way *because of* the victim's race. While this articulation of racial discrimination appears straightforward, it begs the question: How do we know when someone acted *because of* race?

The public debate has been consistent with traditional applications of disparate treatment theory in characterizing the decision to act *because of* race as a conscious choice or intention. It should thus be unsurprising that parties on both sides have tried to offer evidence aimed at establishing the presence or absence of conscious intent....

Recent findings from the fields of psychology and social cognition reveal that implicit biases, often undetectable through introspection and self-reporting, cause us to treat others differently because of their race. To gain a more accurate sense of the role played by implicit biases, we begin by disaggregating the concepts of explicit and implicit biases.

Both explicit and implicit biases are the result of social cognitions. Cognitions are thoughts or feelings, and "[a] social cognition is a thought or feeling about a person or a social group, such as a racial group." Explicit biases are thoughts or feelings that we are aware of and are able to identify through introspection. We commonly, though not always, "agree with and endorse our explicit [biases]."...

Implicit biases "pop[] into mind quickly and automatically without conscious volition." Unlike explicit biases, implicit biases are difficult to identify because of introspective limitations and our own self-monitoring. In fact, we are usually unaware of, or mistaken about, the sources of our implicit biases and the influence they have on our judgment and behavior. Implicit biases may actually include "thought[s] or feeling[s] that we would reject as inaccurate or inappropriate upon self-reflection." This disassociation between implicit and explicit

Contemporary Perspectives on Race

An unfinished mural in a neighborhood in Brooklyn, New York, commemorates Trayvon Martin, a teenager who was shot and killed by neighborhood watch volunteer George Zimmerman in February of 2012. The shooting raised the consciousness of the public about racial profiling and the suspiciousness of young black men based on their appearance. © Richard Levine/Alamy.

biases means that we may honestly believe we hold positive attitudes about a particular racial group, yet we simultaneously hold negative attitudes toward that same group at an implicit level. This explains why being Hispanic, growing up in a multiracial household, having black friends, and honestly professing antiracist ideals does not preclude the possibility that an individual might hold implicit negative attitudes about blacks. . . .

Implicit Bias and Guns

More than twenty studies have measured the impact of race on the decision to shoot. These studies typically involve simulations, which are similar in some respects to video games. The simulations display individuals of various races in a wide variety of contexts, carrying either guns or innocuous items like cell phones or wallets. Participants are instructed to shoot anyone who is armed and to refrain from shooting anyone who is unarmed. Psychologists have found that "[p]articipants are faster and more accurate when shooting an armed black man than an armed white man, and faster and more accurate when responding 'don't shoot' to an unarmed white man than an unarmed black man."

The apparent importance of implicit bias to these studies' findings is striking. [Adam] Benforado explains that "[s]cores on explicit prejudice scales do not correlate with shooter bias. However, experimental participants who demonstrate implicit associations between blacks and weapons are more biased in their shooting behavior." Moreover, black and white participants reveal equivalent levels of shooter bias, suggesting that implicit stereotypes influence shooting decisions more than conscious racial attitudes. Collectively, the science suggests that "blacks face a threat from firearms that is both far more significant and different in character than that posed to whites."

The growing evidence demonstrating that the combination of guns and implicit bias can lead to deadly mistakes makes state intervention imperative. As the primary regulators of guns, states should focus on strategies that defuse this potentially lethal cocktail. . . .

Interestingly, . . . even after trainings effectively improved the accuracy of officer decision making, police officers retained an implicit bias against black men. . . . These results suggest that officers continue to harbor implicit biases but that training helps them reduce the actual consequence of their implicit biases. Given the evidence that training can help reduce the danger that arises from the combination of guns and implicit biases, states should require targeted training for gun owners. . . .

Self-Defense Laws and Implicit Bias

Trayvon's case has drawn national attention to Florida's "stand your ground" self-defense law. . . . Historically, the common law imposed a duty to retreat. As Elizabeth Megale explains,

The duty to retreat protects individuals by requiring an actor to avoid an altercation unless his back is to the wall. This means, if someone attacks a pedestrian on the street, the pedestrian has a duty to run away or otherwise avoid engaging with the attacker, so long as it is reasonably safe to do so.

Stand your ground laws eliminate this duty, and instead allow "an individual to defend against violence without retreating, so long as the individual is lawfully present in that place." Florida is not the only state that has eliminated or reduced the common law duty to retreat. Oklahoma has also adopted a nearly identical "Make My Day" statute, and between 2005 and 2009 over fifteen states adopted some form of the "castle doctrine," which eliminates the duty to retreat before using deadly force under certain circumstances. These types of self-defense laws have troubling implications. Under Florida's law, "anytime one claims to perceive a threat, that individual would be justified in reacting violently, they would have little incentive to diffuse the situation by retreating." Benforado explains that permissive self-defense laws may also alter shooter decision making in a way that increases the impact of implicit bias. A primary concern is that "[o]verly broad Stand Your Ground statutes place lives in danger because a person is permitted to harm, or even kill, another before considering whether an actual threat exists."

Encouraging a culture of permissive self-defense is especially problematic because our implicit biases make it difficult for us to accurately evaluate potentially threatening situations. Studies have shown that identical ambiguous behaviors are more often interpreted as violent when the perpetrator is black, rather than white. Additionally, researchers have found that those with high levels of implicit bias perceive black faces as more hostile than identical white faces. Importantly, "explicit prejudice did not predict when whites saw threatening affect in black faces." Thus, while it is impossible to know whether implicit bias played any role in this case, research shows that implicit biases could have caused Zimmerman to perceive Trayvon Martin as hostile, even if "[t]he media portrayal of George as a racist could not be further from the truth." ...

Thinking About Guns and Race

Trayvon Martin's killing has provided an opportunity for collective reflection on issues of race and violence. However, the bulk of the conversation has focused on explicit racism, ignoring evidence that common implicit biases can also influence real-world behavior. We hope the tragedy will refocus attention on the importance of defusing the deadly combination of implicit bias and guns. Studies show that implicit biases influence shooter decisions, putting blacks at greater risk than whites. States must help defuse implicit bias before it becomes deadly. First, states should consider new gun training programs designed to reduce the power of implicit biases. Second, states should incorporate the latest evidence on implicit bias into their self-defense laws. These interventions may be a small step toward preventing similar tragedies.

An Actor with a Sense of Responsibility to Human and Civil Rights

Stuart Jeffries

Stuart Jeffries is a feature writer and columnist for the Guardian.

Danny Glover is a successful stage and screen actor; however, since his college days in San Francisco, he has also been a political activist. He gradually began to find ways to use his work as an actor as a platform for his reforms. He has been an ambassador for the United Nations Children's Fund (UNICEF), demonstrated against apartheid, and worked on the board of the Black AIDS Institute. He has protested the treatment of prisoners, supported the Occupy movement, and objected publicly to US militarism. He has been especially devoted to political justice in Haiti, a country that underwent a slave rebellion at the end of the eighteenth century but which has since been ruled by oppressive dictators backed by larger, capitalistic countries. He has planned to make an epic film based on the revolution. Glover has also supported women's rights and participated in conferences held by Global Women's Strike.

A few years ago, Danny Glover sat in his car and cried. The Hollywood star and political activist had just heard the news that his friend, Jean-Bertrand Aristide, Haiti's first democratically elected president, had been toppled in a coup backed by the US and France. "It was 28 February 2004 and I sat in that parking lot crying uncontrollably, knowing that we'd have to start building again."

Stuart Jeffries, "Danny Glover: The Good Cop," *Guardian*, May 18, 2012. Copyright © 2012 by the Guardian. All rights reserved. Reproduced by permission.

Glover's Work for Haiti

Glover fixes me with tired eyes as we sit in an upstairs room of the Crossroads Women's Centre in London's Kentish Town on a rainy Saturday afternoon. He has just flown in from the US and the same evening will give a speech at the centre during a fund-raiser for the Haiti Emergency Relief Fund.

In the years since Aristide was ousted, Haiti has suffered floods, mudslides, hurricanes, an earthquake in 2010 that killed tens of thousands, followed by a cholera outbreak that killed nearly 6,000. Infrastructure has collapsed, gang violence remains rife and the UN [United Nations] has described the human rights situation as "catastrophic".

"When I talk about Haiti, it breaks my heart," says Glover. "Yet when I think about the Haitian people's resilience, it heals my heart at the same time."

This is Glover's great theme and his deepest conviction: that there is something special and indomitable about the Haitian people. "You've got to know your history," says Glover. "The great American abolitionist Frederick Douglass said the Haitian revolution was the first victory against the worldwide system of slavery. Not Wilberforce [referring to William Wilberforce, the English leader of the movement to abolish slave trade]. Wilberforce may have understood that, in an emerging capitalist society, slavery had gone through its evolutionary purpose, but it was the Haitians who struck the first blow.

"I know that blood runs through them from that time. And since the moment they organised that revolution, they have been defeated on, they've been undermined, yet they keep organising. And you look in their faces and they could well have been the faces that stood facing Napoleon's [Bonaparte's] army."

A Slave Revolt and a Revolution (1791–1804)

Glover found out about the 1791–1804 Haitian revolution led by Toussaint L'Ouverture in the early 1970s when he read *The*

Contemporary Perspectives on Race

Black Jacobins by C.L.R. James, the Trinidadian socialist historian (and sometime Manchester *Guardian* cricket correspondent). By that time, Glover was already a protest veteran who, as a member of the black students' union at San Francisco State University, had participated in a five-month strike to establish a black studies department. But it made an enormous impact on him.

For more than 30 years, Glover has been trying to make a biopic about the leader of the Haitian revolution. True, the story of L'Ouverture has been told before, notably in a play by C.L.R. James that was staged in London's West End in 1936 starring Paul Robeson, and more recently in a French TV series starring Haitian actor Jimmy Jean-Louis. But Glover believes his treatment will be the first to "have the epic scale these events require".

But when will we see this directorial debut? In 2006, Glover assembled a cast including Wesley Snipes, Angela Bassett, Chiwetel Ejiofor and Mos Def, and planned to shoot his film in South Africa and Venezuela, thanks to $18m [million] (£11m) from one of Glover's heroes, Venezuelan president Hugo Chávez. Six years on, filming has not started. "We'll get the film done," says Glover. "We came so close so many times, you could almost taste it, man. We came that close and we're going to do it."

Why is the project so important to him? "Imagine a revolt where all those people who were enslaved and dispossessed in Africa, America and round the world, heard what had happened? You imagine what that meant to them?"

Glover's Support of a Controversial Leader

Glover met Aristide in 1992 when the former Catholic priest was ousted as president for the first time. Shortly after that coup, Glover was flying to Oakland to attend a rally for him. "I still had my makeup on when I got to my seat on the flight at Burbank airport. I look over to my right and there he is. I said: 'President Aristide! I'm going to a rally for you!' He always says: 'The look on your face when you saw me.' He's been my brother and friend since that moment."

What about Aristide's alleged human rights abuses and corruption? "He's a human being—none of us is perfect. But whatever he has done, he has never done with the intention of harming his people. He built more schools than at any time since the revolution; he improved healthcare. Each time he's come back, he's put his life in danger. He could have stayed in exile."

But, to the disappointment of many—including Barack Obama—Aristide didn't. Last year [2011], Glover flew with Aristide from South African exile to Port-au-Prince [the capital of Haiti]. "It's shameful the South Africans may have worked with US and France to stop him returning," says Glover. When they arrived at Port-au-Prince, Glover was in Aristide's car as they drove from the airport. "That car could only move as fast as people around allowed it. That was one of the most moving things in my life. That's one story I'm going to tell my grandson."

Does his country's stance on Haiti outrage him? "A great deal of US policy is centred around exclusion and destabilisation. You take the largest party out of the process [Aristide's Fanmi Lavalas]—what kind of an election is that? We have a very interesting dilemma in Haiti at the moment. The current president [Michel] Martelly was the choice of the State Department and France and Canada, but if you'd had a free election, he would never have been elected."

How does he feel now about the US's first black president whose 2008 candidacy he endorsed? Glover laughs. "I'm not into personality worship. It's essential that you clearly denounce those things you disagree with. Everything he has done in terms of war, I'm opposed to. How much of that is him following the line and how much his own thought processes, we don't know. The bottom line is I think he's a good man."

Both Actor and Political Activist

Glover recalls that in 2002 or 2003, as a member of the board of the Algebra Project, a US scheme to improve math skills among disadvantaged children, he took part in a discussion on the future of education in Chicago. "A young state senator walked in and got involved in the discussion. I have to believe he'd come there because of a sincere desire to learn more and do something about that. He hasn't delivered. We're still waiting."

Glover and I are sharing a sofa in an upstairs room. Below there's a conference going on called Invest in Caring Not Capitalism: The Wages for Housework Campaign 40 Years On. It's been organised by a group called Global Women's Strike, one of whose leading members is Selma James, women's rights campaigner and C.L.R. James's widow, who is promoting her new book *Sex, Race, and Class—The Perspective of Winning: A Selection of Writings 1952–2011*.

Glover, despite his gender, feels at home. "Like Selma was saying, I'm into building caring as opposed to capitalism." The world knows Glover as Detective Roger Murtaugh in the *Lethal Weapon* film franchise, as the brutish husband Albert Johnson in *The Color Purple*, as maverick alien-battling narcotics cop Michael Harrigan in *Predator 2*, as the laughably impotent US president in the eco-disaster movie *2012* and as Nelson Mandela in the TV movie. He's just about to start work on Stephen Frears' HBO film about Muhammad Ali's refusal to fight in Vietnam in which he will play Thurgood Marshall, the first African American US Supreme Court judge.

But it also knows him as an actor who has said "hey" to radical political intervention activism more times than Angelina Jolie, George Clooney, Mark Ruffalo and Sean Penn com-

Actor Danny Glover is an outspoken activist for many causes worldwide. In this photo, he is seen speaking in Hamtramck, Michigan, at a rally to save American automobile manufacturing jobs that was organized by the United Steelworkers and the Alliance for American Manufacturing. © Jim West/Alamy.

Contemporary Perspectives on Race

bined. He's regularly on picket lines, campaigning for prisoners, speaking against US militarism and giving talks at Occupy protests. In 2004, he was arrested outside the Sudanese embassy in Washington [DC] during a protest about Darfur. In 2010, he called on all actors at the 2010 Academy Awards to boycott Hugo Boss in support of a pay dispute. He's been an ambassador for Unicef [the United Nations Children's Fund], fought against apartheid through a campaign group called the TransAfrica Forum and sits on the boards of several groups, including the Black AIDS Institute and the Jazz Foundation of America.

At 65, he could readily spend weekends dozing poolside in California rather than busting his hump at a fund-raiser in this rain-soaked dime of a country. Where did that enduring political commitment come from? Glover locates it in January 1959 when he witnessed how his parents, Carrie and James, both postal workers, celebrated the Cuban revolution with their union. "I was a 12-year-old kid watching these workers celebrate. I never forgot that. I was around that union a lot and surreptitiously, vicariously listened to what they talked about, how they would strategise about an action. All that was part of my acculturation as a child."...

But how did this rad activist become a movie star and befriend one of Hollywood's most disreputable conservatives, Mel Gibson? "I never thought I was going to be a Hollywood star." During his 20s and early 30s he worked in community development projects in San Francisco. Stage acting was a sideline. Then he discovered Athol Fugard, the South African writer best known for [German playwright and director Bertolt] Brecht-inflected anti-apartheid plays. "Once I started doing Fugard, I became more entrenched in my political work. I could see how you could use your work as an actor as a platform. He became my writer."

In 1982, he was seen, aged 36, in an off-Broadway production of Fugard's *Master Harold ... and the Boys* by Robert

Benton. The film director cast Glover in his 1984 Depression-era picture *Places in the Heart* as a black hobo turned farmhand opposite Sally Field, who won an Oscar for her performance as a Texan widow struggling to run the family farm. His movie career then took off. The following year he starred opposite Whoopi Goldberg in Steven Spielberg's adaptation of Alice Walker's novel *The Color Purple*, as Celie's abusive husband....

Glover yawns. "Are we good?" he asks, ever avuncular. "Because I think I'm done." He needs a nap before he makes his fund-raising speech for Haiti in the evening.

Downstairs, the afternoon's panel discussion about the struggles against poverty, ecological devastation, military occupation, war, asylum and immigration is in full flow. Glover won't be part of it, even though his radical credentials are unimpeachable. A few minutes later, I return to find all 6ft 4in of him curled up on that sofa asleep. It would have been a shame to wake him.

Alabama Looks for Way to Pardon Scottsboro Boys

Phillip Rawls

Phillip Rawls, an Associated Press reporter in Montgomery, Alabama, covers politics and state government.

A notorious case of racial injustice beginning in 1931, with which Langston Hughes was involved, surfaced again in 2012. In that year, a group of African Americans, some of whom lived in Scottsboro, Alabama, began attempts to secure posthumous pardons for men who had been wrongly imprisoned for rape even though medical evidence had long ago confirmed that they were innocent. The process of obtaining the pardons is not an easy task, despite the governor of Alabama's declaration that he would issue the pardon if he was permitted to do so. However, he said, he could not pardon the Scottsboro defendants because the rules to the Alabama Board of Pardons and Paroles will not allow posthumous pardons. To complicate matters, the legislature must agree to change the rules of the board. However, more than eighty years after the multiple convictions, despite the technicalities, the plan has strong governmental support.

Many years ago, public opinion deemed the black Scottsboro Boys innocent of raping two white women. Making that official is taking decades longer.

Only one of the nine Scottsboro Boys was formally pardoned by Alabama before dying. State officials would like to clear the names of the other eight, but figuring out how to rewrite history after 81 years is proving difficult.

Phillip Rawls, "Alabama Looks for Way to Pardon Scottsboro Boys," Associated Press, September 2, 2012. Copyright © 2012 by The Associated Press. All rights reserved. Reproduced by permission.

Gov. Robert Bentley said he would issue a pardon if state law allowed him to do so, but it doesn't.

"We need to right any wrongs that have occurred in the past as best we can. This was a long time ago, and we have moved so far in this state," he said.

The state Board of Pardons and Paroles issued a pardon in 1976 to the only Scottsboro Boy who was known to still be alive, Clarence Norris. But the board's rules don't allow posthumous pardons, and changing those rules could take months.

Some legislators plan to propose a resolution declaring the eight cleared in the view of the state, but it can't be considered until the legislature's next meeting, scheduled for February.

"It shouldn't be so hard," said Sheila Washington, founder of the Scottsboro Boys Museum and Cultural Center in Scottsboro.

The museum chronicles how race and sex intersected in the segregated South on March 25, 1931, when a sheriff's posse stopped a train at Paint Rock, Ala. Nine black teenagers who were hoboing thought they were being arrested for fighting with whites on the train. Instead, they were accused of gang-raping two white women who were also riding the freight train.

The nine, from Georgia and Tennessee, went on trial in Scottsboro. All but the youngest received a death sentence but later won new trials. One of the women recanted her story. Five of the Scottsboro Boys eventually had the rape charges dropped, while four were convicted.

The case resulted in two significant U.S. Supreme Court decisions saying that criminal defendants are entitled to effective counsel and that blacks can't be systematically excluded from criminal juries.

When Norris obtained his pardon in 1976 with the support of then Gov. George C. Wallace, there was talk of trying to do something for Andy and Roy Wright, Haywood Patterson, Olen Montgomery, Charlie Weems, Ozie Powell, William Roberson and Eugene Williams. Nothing happened, and then little was said after Norris died in 1989.

Washington and other volunteers opened the Scottsboro Boys Museum in an old church in 2010 and brought the case to the attention of tourists visiting civil rights attractions in the South. She recently contacted the parole board and governor to try to get the other eight Scottsboro Boys exonerated. Prominent defense lawyers, legislators and others have endorsed her efforts.

The governor said he's looking to the parole board for action. Parole board attorney Greg Griffin said the board is looking at whether it has the legal authority to pass a resolution saying that if the eight were still alive, they would have been granted pardons.

A state representative from Scottsboro who raised money to start the museum and the longest serving black member of the legislature are working on resolutions to proclaim the Scottsboro Boys exonerated in the state's eyes.

Democratic Rep. John Robinson of Scottsboro and Democratic Rep. Alvin Holmes of Montgomery said they will have resolutions ready for the next legislative session.

Robinson grew up 20 miles away on Sand Mountain and remembers hearing stories about the Scottsboro Boys. One particular story about an unsuccessful lynch mob stands out in his mind.

"People came off Sand Mountain with rifles and shotguns and came over to Scottsboro to lynch the Scottsboro Boys. It was quite a time," he said.

Robinson not only helped raise money for the museum, he lives in the house that belonged to one of the physicians who examined the two women for evidence of rape.

Even though 81 years have passed, Robinson and Holmes said it's still important for the state to write one more chapter in the story of the Scottsboro Boys.

"If a wrong has been done—and everyone agrees that a wrong has been done—we can say we are sorry for it. It will help our image as a state," Robinson said.

Washington said it's never too late to remove the shame that was unfairly placed on the names of the Scottsboro Boys.

"It will change the course of history," she said.

For Further Discussion

1. Discuss Hughes's realizations about race and politics throughout his early life. Reference viewpoints by R. Baxter Miller and Arnold Rampersad to formulate your answer.
2. What music influenced Hughes and in what way? Reference viewpoints by Onwuchekwa Jemie and Martha Cobb to formulate your answer. From what you have read and seen in your own experience, how would Hughes have regarded rap and hip hop?
3. What conclusions can you draw from his poems about Hughes's personal religion? Reference his poems as well as the viewpoint by Mary Beth Culp to formulate your answer.
4. Discuss Hughes's politics. Where do you think he would have fit in the present political scene? Reference his poems as well as viewpoints by Raymond Smith, W. Jason Miller, and Christopher C. DeSantis to formulate your answer.
5. In your opinion, would Hughes have been involved in racial problems today, and would he have approved of the work of Danny Glover? Reference viewpoints by Wendy R. Weiser and Lawrence Norden, Stuart Jeffries, and Jonathan Feingold and Karen Lorang to formulate your answer.
6. Looking over the contemporary viewpoints and the racial issues discussed in chapter three, write a short poem in the manner of one of Hughes's poems.

For Further Reading

Arna Bontemps, *Drums at Dusk*. New York: Macmillan, 1939.

Countee Cullen, *My Soul's High Song: The Collected Writings of Countee Cullen, Voice of the American Renaissance*, Gerald Early, ed. New York: Doubleday, 1991.

W.E.B. Du Bois, *The Souls of Black Folk: Essays and Sketches*. Chicago, IL: A.C. McClurg & Co., 1903.

Langston Hughes, *The Collected Poems of Langston Hughes*, Arnold Rampersad, ed. New York: Knopf, 1994.

Langston Hughes, *I Wonder as I Wander: An Autobiographical Journey*. New York: Thunder's Mouth Press, 1956.

Langston Hughes, *Mulatto*. 1935.

Langston Hughes, *Not Without Laughter*. New York: Knopf, 1930.

Langston Hughes, *Scottsboro Limited*. New York: Golden Stair Press, 1932.

Langston Hughes, *Simple Speaks His Mind*. New York: Simon & Schuster, 1950.

Langston Hughes, *Tambourines to Glory: A Novel*. New York: John Day, 1958.

Alain Locke, *The Works of Alain Locke*, Charles Molesworth, ed. New York: Oxford University Press, 2012.

Bibliography

Books

Amiri Baraka	*Black Music.* New York: Akashic Books, 2010.
Richard K. Barksdale	*Langston Hughes: The Poet and His Critics.* Chicago, IL: American Library Association, 1977.
Emily Bernard, ed.	*Remember Me to Harlem: The Letters of Langston Hughes and Carl Van Vechten, 1925–1964.* New York: Knopf, 2001.
Faith Berry	*Langston Hughes: Before and Beyond Harlem.* Westport, CT: Lawrence Hill, 1983.
Pat E. Bonner	*Sassy Jazz and Slo' Draggin' Blues: Music in the Poetry of Langston Hughes.* New York: P. Lange, 2000.
James E. Emmanuel	*Langston Hughes.* New York: Twayne, 1967.
James S. Haskins	*Always Movin' On: The Life of Langston Hughes.* Trenton, NJ: Africa World Press, 1993.
Robin D.G. Kelley	*Race Rebels: Culture, Politics, and the Black Working Class.* New York: Free Press, 1994.

David M. Kennedy	*Don't Shoot: One Man, a Street Fellowship, and the End of Violence in Inner-City America*. New York: Bloomsbury USA, 2011.
Joseph McLaren	*Langston Hughes: Folk Dramatist in the Protest Tradition, 1921–1943*. Westport, CT: Greenwood Press, 1997.
Therman B. O'Daniel, ed.	*Langston Hughes: Black Genius: A Critical Evaluation*. New York: Morrow, 1971.
Jonathan Scott	*Socialist Joy in the Writing of Langston Hughes*. Columbia: University of Missouri Press, 2006.
Steven C. Tracy	*Langston Hughes and the Blues*. Urbana: University of Illinois Press, 1988.
C. James Trotman, ed.	*Langston Hughes: The Man, His Art, and His Continuing Influence*. New York: Garland, 1995.
Cornel West with David Ritz	*Brother West: Living and Loving Out Loud*. New York: Smiley Books, 2009.

Periodicals

Edward O. Ako	"Langston Hughes and the Négritude Movement: A Study in Literary Influences," *College Language Association Journal*, vol. 28, September 1984, pp. 46–56.

Bibliography

George H. Bass	"Five Stories About a Man Named Hughes: A Critical Reflection," *The Langston Hughes Review*, vol. 1, Spring 1982, pp. 1–12.
Juda Bennett	"Multiple Passings and the Double Death of Langston Hughes," *Biography*, vol. 23, no. 4, Fall 2000, pp. 670–693.
Sundiata Keita Cha-Jua	"'Lest Harlem Sees Red': Race and Class Themes in the Poetry of Langston Hughes, 1920–1942," *Afro-Americans in New York Life and History*, vol. 19, no. 2, July 31, 1995.
Arthur P. Davis	"Langston Hughes: Cool Poet," *CLA Journal*, vol. 11, no. 4, June 1968, pp. 280–296.
Walter C. Farrell Jr. and Patricia A. Johnson	"Poetic Interpretations of Urban Black Folk Culture: Langston Hughes and the 'Bebop Era,'" *Ethnic Literature and Cultural Consciousness*, vol. 8, no. 3, Fall 1981, pp. 57–72.
Thurmon Garner and Carolyn Calloway-Thomas	"Langston Hughes' Message for the Black Masses," *Communications Quarterly*, vol. 39, no. 2, Spring 1991, pp. 164–177.
Calvin Hernton	"The Poetic Consciousness of Langston Hughes from Affirmation to Revolution," *Langston Hughes Review*, vol. 12, no. 1, Spring 1993, pp. 2–9.

Theodore R. Hudson	"Langston Hughes' Last Volume of Verse," *CLA Journal*, vol. 11, June 1968, pp. 280–290.
Jon Hurwitz and Mark Peffley	"Public Perceptions of Race and Crime: The Role of Racial Stereotypes," *American Journal of Political Science*, vol. 41, no. 2, April 1997, pp. 375–401.
Scott Keyes, Ian Millhiser, Tobin Van Ostern, and Abraham White	"Voter Suppression Disenfranchises Millions," *New Political Spaces*, vol. 19, no. 1, 2012.
Margaret Larkin	"A Poet for the People: A Review," *Opportunity*, vol. 3, 1927, pp. 84–95.
Delita Martin	"Langston Hughes's Use of the Blues," *CLA Journal*, vol. 22, no. 2, December 1978, pp. 151–159.
Milton Meltzer	"Harlem Poet: Langston Hughes Comes to Harlem," *Cobblestone*, vol. 12, no. 2, February 1991, p. 10.
Clarence Page	"Talk of 'The Plan' Is a Paranoid View of Black Problems," *Chicago Tribune*, January 24, 1990.
Leonard Pitts, Jr.	"The Same Old Hate, This Time on a Bumper Sticker," *Tampa Bay Times*, September 22, 2012.
James Presley	"The American Dream of Langston Hughes," *Southwest Review*, vol. 48, no. 4, Fall 1963, pp. 380–386.

Kenneth Rexroth	"Jazz Poetry," *Nation*, vol. 186, March 28, 1958, pp. 282–283.
Michael Thurston	"Black Christ, Red Flag: Langston Hughes on Scottsboro," *College Literature*, vol. 22, no. 3, October 1995, pp. 30–49.
Sherley Anne Williams	"Langston Hughes and the Negro Renaissance: 'Harlem Literati in the Twenties,'" *Langston Hughes Review*, vol. 9, no. 2, Fall 1985.

Index

A

Abernethy, Milton, 22
Abolitionists and Hughes' ancestors, 9, 28, 29, 31–32, *33*
Academy Awards, 141
"Acceptance" (Hughes), 66
Africa
    idealization, 39–40
    imagery in "The Negro Speaks of Rivers," 45–46, 94–95
    influence of folklore and music, 9, 56, 62
    literature, 98
    Pan-Africanism, 26
    trips, 16, 26, 82, 87–88, 98
African American culture
    affirmation of in Hughes' works, 85–87
    childhood exposure, 33–35
    Hughes' need to appease, 36
    influence on Hughes, 9, 49, 56–58, 61–62, 65, 89–90
    subject in Hughes' poetry, 20, 55–62
    See also African American literature; African Americans
African American literature
    artistic process, 61–62
    biracial stereotypes, 74–77
    Black Orpheus (magazine), 98
    folklore, 9, 49, 56, 57, 61–62, 65, 89–90
    Harlem Renaissance, 9–10, 16–17, 19, 49, 83, 99–100
    Hughes' criticisms, 108
    origins and traditions, 38, 39, 55–56, 58
    religion, 65–66
    See also African American culture; Harlem Renaissance
African Americans
    criticism of leadership, 105–108
    voting laws are diminishing rights, 117–125
African literature, 98
Afro-French literature, 62
Afro-Hispanic literature, 62
AIDS, 135, 141
Alabama, A&M Institute incident, 105–106
Algebra Project, 139
Ali, Muhammad, 139
Alliance for American Manufacturing, 140
Allusion, 26, 93
A&M Institute, 105–106
America. *See* United States
America First Party, 68
American Academy of Arts and Letters prize, 25
American South. *See* The South
American Writers' Congress (1935), 107–108
Anti-capitalism, 48
Anti-communism
    censorship of Hughes' works, 91–98
    Senate investigation, 11, 25, 91, 93–94, *107*, 112–114
Anti-military protests, 133, 138, 141
Apartheid, 135

Index

Aristide, Jean-Bertrand, 135, 137–138
Aristotle, 39
"As I Grew Older" (Hughes), 86
Ask Your Mama (Hughes), 26
Atlanta University, 25
Atlanta World (newspaper), 71
"August 19th . . . A Poem for Clarence Norris" (Hughes), 11
"Aunt Sue's Stories" (Hughes), 9
Autocitation, 93
Automobile industry, 140

B

Baker, Josephine, 17
Baldwin, James, 39
"The Ballad of the Landlord" (Hughes), 42
Baraka, Amiri, 38–39, 52
Bassett, Angela, 137
Bates, Ruby, 101, 102
    See also Scottsboro incident
Beier, Ulli, 98
Benforado, Adam, 132, 133
Bennett, Mike, 121
Bentley, Robert, 143–145
Benton, Robert, 141–142
Berger, Phil, 125
The Best of Simple (Hughes), 25–26
Bethune, Mary McLeod, 83
Bias, explicit, 130–131, 134
Bias, implicit, 126–134
"Bible Belt" (Hughes), 11
"Big Meeting" (Hughes), 69–70
The Big Sea (Hughes), 80, 99–100
Biracialism
    "Cross," 21, 73, 75–76
    Hughes family, 28, 29, 87–88
    "I, Too," 41, 42–45, 84
    "Mulatto," 21, 76–80
    parental rejection theme, 21, 73–81
    stereotypes, 74–77
"The Bitter River" (Hughes), 46–47, 98
Black AIDS Institute, 135, 141
Black Arts movement, 16–17
Black colleges, 22, 105–106
Black Consciousness movement, 39
Black culture. *See* African American culture
The Black Jacobins (James), 136–137
Black Mountain School, 52
Black Orpheus (magazine), 98
Blesh, Rudi, 26
"Blue Bayou" (Hughes), 94, 97
The Blue Devils of Nada (Murray), 53
Blues music
    "Dream Variations," 51–52
    first experiences, 34–35, 50
    freedom imagery, 51
    "Homesick Blues," 50
    "I, Too," 41, 42–44
    influence on Baraka, 52
    influence on Hughes, 9–10, 17, 19–21, 49–53, 55, *58*, 60–61
    "Midwinter Blues," 50–51
    "Misery," 60–61
    "Mother to Son," 41–42
    "The Negro Mother," 41–42
    "The Negro Speaks of Rivers," 41
    "Proem," 40–41
    "The Weary Blues," 19–20, 35, 49, 84–85

155

"Blues, Poetry, and the New Music" (Baraka), 52
Bogdanoff, Ellyn, 121
Bonds, Hughes' work for U.S. Defense, 25
"Bound No'th Blues" (Hughes), 97
Boy Scouts of America, 28, 32
Boyd (Hughes' character), 26
Brennan Center for Justice, 117, 118, 121
Brooks, Gwendolyn, 17
"Brown America in Jail: Kilby" (Hughes), 102–103
Brown, Claude, 52–53
Brown, John, 33
    Hughes' family connections, 9, 18, 28, 29, 31–32
    imagery in "Scottsboro," 47
Brown, Major, 105–106
Brown, Sterling A., 74
Browning, Kurt S., 122
Buttita, Anthony, 22

C

California voting laws, 120
Call-and-response pattern, 19
Canada and Haiti relations, 138
Capitalism, criticisms, 48, 99–114
    See also Communism
"Castle doctrine," 133
    See also "Stand your ground" laws and implicit bias
Censorship
    jazz in the Soviet Union, 24
    lynching poems, 91–98
"Chant for May Day" (Hughes), 11
Chávez, Hugo, 137
Chicago Defender, 25, 110–111
Chicago, Illinois, 25
Chicago Renaissance, 50
Children, rejection of biracial, 21, 73–81
China visit, 24
Christ imagery
    "Big Meeting," 69
    Christ child poems, 66
    "Christ in Alabama," 47–48, 70–71
    "Feet o' Jesus," 60
    "Goodbye Christ," 67–68
    lynching poems, 38, 47–48, 66, 70–72
    "Ma Lord," 68–69
    "A New Song", 66–67
    "Song for a Dark Girl," 71–72
    symbol of black suffering, 68–71
"Christ in Alabama" (Hughes)
    censorship, 98
    martyr imagery, 47–48, 70–71
    narrative structure, 94
    as reaction to visit to the South, 10, 22, 71
    readings, 22, 71
Christianity. See Religion
Church. See Religion
Church music influence on Hughes, 9, 28, 35
Civil Rights activism, 135–142
    See also Racism; Segregation
Clark, Homer, 18
Cleaver, Eldridge, 39
Clown stereotype, 40
Cobb, Martha, 55–62
Cognitions and bias, 130
Cohn, Roy, 113
Colleges and universities
    enrollment at Lincoln University, 21

Hughes' criticisms, 22, 105–106
political protests, 137
positions, 25
speaking tour, 21–22, 71, 83, 88–89, 102
The Color Purple (film), 139, 142
Colorado trip, 18, 31
Communism
  Hughes' endorsement, 11, 16, 23, 64, 91–92, 99, 101, 110–112
  Hughes' renunciation, 112–114
  Scottsboro incident, 101, 103
  Senate investigation, 11, 25, 91, 93–94, *107,* 112–114
  Soviet Union trip, 11, 16, 23–24, 110–112
  as subject in Hughes' work, 10, 48, 67–68, 110–112
Concealed weapon licenses, 123
Congo River, 45–46, 94–95
Consciousness, dual, 83–85
Contempo (University of North Carolina magazine), 22
Corey, Angela, 128
"Cowards from the Colleges" (Hughes), 105–106
Crisis (magazine)
  "Cowards from the Colleges," 105–106
  "The Negro Speaks of Rivers," 56
  "Not for Publication," 98
  "The South," 88–89
"Cross" (Hughes), 21, 73, 75–76
Cuba
  literature, 56, 62
  Revolution, 141

Cullen, Countee, 16, 49
Culp, Mary Beth, 64–72

D

Darfur protests, 141
Darrow, Clarence, 21
Davis, Arthur P., 73–81
Davis, Jim, 124–125
The Dead Lecturer (Baraka), 52
Def, Mos, 137
Derricotte, Juliette, 71, 105
DeSantis, Christopher C., 99–114
Dessa Rose (Williams), 52
Diakhaté, Lamine, 26–27
Dialect
  influence on Hughes' works, 89
  Jesse B. Simple stories, 26
Dillard, Mary J., 32
Dirksen, Everett, 113–114
Disabled voters, 118–120
Discrimination. *See* Racism; Segregation
"Disillusion" (Hughes), 40
Disparate treatment theory, 130
Dix, Larry, 119–120
Dodat, François, 27
"Doubleness" in Hughes' works, 83–85
Douglas, Aaron, 17
Douglass, Frederick, 136
"Dream Variations" (Hughes), 51–52
Du Bois, W.E.B., *43*
  dedications, *43,* 46
  dual consciousness, 83–84
  tradition of African American literature, 39, 56, 58
Dunbar, Paul Laurence, 40

E

Early voting restrictions, 117, 123–125
Education
    Glover, Danny, 139
    Hughes, 21, 28, 30–31, 32, 35–36
    Hughes' criticism of black colleges, 22, 105–106
    Hughes' parents, 17
    speaking tours, colleges, 21–22, 71, 83, 88–89, 102
Ejiofor, Chiwetel, 137
Elderly and voting laws, 117
Ellison, Ralph, 39
"Epilogue." *See* "I, Too" (Hughes)
Evans, Mari, 17
Explicit bias, 130–131, 134

F

Fanmi Lavalas (Haitian political party), 138
Fascism, 16, 24
Fathers' rejection of biracial children, 21, 73–81
FBI security index, 26
"Feet o' Jesus" (Hughes), 60
Feingold, Jonathan, 126–134
Field, Sally, 142
Fine Clothes to the Jew (Hughes), 21, 85, 106
The First Book of Negroes (Hughes), 25
Fisk University. *See* Derricotte, Juliette
Florida
    implicit bias in Trayvon Martin shooting, 126–134
    "stand your ground" law, 128, 132–134
    voting laws, 117, 120–122, 123–124
Folklore
    influence on Hughes, 9, 49, 56, 57, 61–62, 89–90
    interests, 65
Foster, Eli S., 30
France
    Haiti relations, 138
    trip, 26
Freaks, Stephen, 139
Freedom of expression in Soviet Union, 23, 24, 111
"Freedom's Plow" (Hughes), 11
From the Virginia Plantation to the National Capital (Langston), 17
Fugard, Athol, 141–142

G

Gandhi, Mohandas K., 47
Georgia, 71, 103–104, 105
Gibson, Mel, 141
Global Women's Strike, 135, 139
Glover, Danny, 135–142, *140*
"God Bless the Child That's Got His Own" (Holiday), 28–29
Goldberg, Whoopi, 142
Good Morning Revolution (Hughes), 102–103, 105–106, 107–108, 110–111
"Goodbye Christ" (Hughes), 10, 67–68, 109–110
Gospel music. *See* Church music influence on Hughes; Spirituals
"Governor Fires Dean" (Hughes), 11

Index

Great Depression
    effect on Harlem Renaissance, 10, 50, 100
    effect on Hughes, 10, 83, 108
Great Migration, 26, 89, 94, 97
Green, Paul, 22
Griffin, Greg, 145
Gronstal, Mike, 120
Guillén, Nicolás, 56, 62
Guns
    implicit bias in shootings, 126–127, 131–132
    licenses as voter IDs, 123

H

Haiti
    Glover, Danny, 135–138
    Hughes' ancestry, 29
    literature, 56, 62
    Revolution (1791–1804), 136–137
Hampton Institute, 71, 105–106
Harlem Renaissance
    end, 99–100
    Hughes as part, 16–17, 19, 49, 83
    themes, 9–10
Harmon Award, 100
Harpers Ferry raid (1859), 9, 18, 28, 29, 31–32, *33*
Hayes, Roland, 103–104
Henderson, Stephen, 51, 58–61
"Here To Yonder" column (Hughes), 110–111
"Hey! Hey!" (Hughes), 85
Himes, Chester, 39
Hispanics and voting laws, 117–125
Historical imagery
    lynching poems, 92–97
"The Negro Speaks of Rivers" (Hughes), 45–46, 50, 85, 94–96
HIV/AIDS, 135, 141
Holiday, Billie, 28–29
Holmes, Alvin, 145–146
"Homesick Blues" (Hughes), 50
Hoodies (clothing), 128
Hughes, Carrie Langston, 17, 18, 30, 31
Hughes, James Mercer Langston. *See* Hughes, Langston
Hughes, James Nathaniel
    abandonment of family, 16, 18, 80
    birth of Hughes, 17
    conflict with Hughes, 80–81
    death, 24
    education, 17
    Mexico, 18, 80–81
    rejection of race, 80–81, 89
Hughes, Langston
    artist announcement, 56–57
    artistic process, 61–62
    biography, 16–27
    birth, 56
    childhood, 9, 17–19, 28, 29–36
    education, 21, 28, 30–31, 32, 35–36
    fame, 16–17, 24–26
    family history, 9, 18, 28, 29, 31–32, *33*
    images, *20, 78, 107*
    influence and legacy on other writers, 52, 56
    lack of personal content in works, 85, 86, 92
    Senate investigation, 11, 25, 91, 93–94, *107,* 112–114
    sexuality, 29
    suicidal thoughts, 81

Hugo Boss, 141
Human rights in Haiti, 138
Hurston, Zora Neale, 49

I

"I Hear America Singing" (Whitman), 44–45
"I, Too" (Hughes), 41, 42–45, 84
I Wonder as I Wander (Hughes), 71, 101, 102
Identification, voter, 117, 118, 119–120, 122–123
Illinois voting laws, 120
Imagism, 50
Implicit bias, 126–134
International Labor Defense, 101
Iowa State Association of County Auditors (ISACA), 120
Iowa voting laws, 119, 120
Irony
   Ask Your Mama, 26
   "black-white" type, 85
   "Cross," 78–79
   "Goodbye Christ," 67
   as Hughes' characteristic, 90
   A New Song, 24
   radical writings, 100, 102
   Scottsboro incident, 102
   "Song for a Dark Girl," 72
ISACA (Iowa State Association of County Auditors), 120

J

Jahn, Janheinz, 98
James, C.L.R., 137
James, Selma, 139
Janssen, Charlie, 119
Japan visit, 24
Jazz Foundation of America, 141

Jazz music
   freedom imagery, 51
   Glover, Danny, 141
   influence on Baraka, 52
   influence on Hughes, 9–10, 17, 26, *58*, 85
   Soviet ban, 24
Jean-Louis, Jimmy, 137
Jeffries, Stuart, 135–142
Jemie, Onwuchekwa, 38–48
Jesse B. Simple. *See* Simple, Jesse B. (Hughes character)
Jesus Christ. *See* Christ imagery
Jews, Soviet, 24
Jim Crow laws. *See* Racism; Segregation
Jim Crow "row," 35–36
Joans, Ted, 17
John Brown raid. *See* Brown, John; Harpers Ferry raid (1859)
Johnson, Guy B., 22
Johnson, Helene, 49
Johnson, James Weldon, 21
Jones, LeRoi. *See* Baraka, Amiri
Joplin, Missouri, 17
"Judgment Day" (Hughes), 64, 66
"Justice" (Hughes), 25, 47

K

Kansas City, Missouri, 34–35, 50
Katz, Bill, 26
Koestler, Arthur, 23
Komunyakaa, Yusef, 49–53
Korea, 24
"Ku Klux Klan" (Hughes), 11

L

Laboratory School University of Chicago, 25

Index

Ladder imagery, 41–42
Langston, Carrie. *See* Hughes, Carrie Langston
Langston, Charles Howard, 17, 32
The Langston Hughes Reader, 98
Langston Hughes Review, 9
Langston Hughes Society, 9
Langston, John Mercer, 17
Langston, Mary Leary
    Hughes' childhood, 18, 29–30, 31–36
    voice in Hughes' works, 55, 59–60
Lawrence, Kansas, 18, 28, 31–36, 78
League of Struggle for Negro Rights, 101
"Lenin" (Hughes), 11, 112
Lenin, Vladimir
    Hughes' reading, 11
    as subject in Hughes' work, 11, 68, 110, 112
"Let America Be America Again" (Hughes), 25
Lethal Weapon, 139
The Life of Langston Hughes (Rampersad), 50
Lincoln University, 21
Lindsay, Vachel, 50
Lorang, Karen, 126–134
Lynching attempt of Scottsboro accused, 145
Lynching poems
    "The Bitter River," 46–47, 98
    "Blue Bayou," 94, 97
    censorship, 91–98
    Christ imagery, 38, 47–48, 66, 70–72
    "Christ in Alabama," 10, 22, 47–48, 70–71, 94, 98
    "Lynching Song," 94
    "The Negro Speaks of Rivers," 94
    "Proem," 40, 92–93, 97
    "Silhouette," 94, 97
    as subject in Hughes' work, 10, 38, 70–72, 91–98
    "Three Lynching Songs," 98
"Lynching Song" (Hughes), 94

M

"Ma Lord" (Hughes), 68–69
Marshall, Thurgood, 139
Martelly, Michel, 138
Martin, Trayvon, 126–134, *131*
Marx, Karl, 11, 68, 110
Marxism. *See* Communism
Mason, Charlotte, 106–107
Master Harold . . . and the Boys (Fugard), 141–142
McCarthy, Joseph, 25, 112
    See also Senate Permanent Subcommittee on Investigations (1953)
McKay, Claude, 49–50
Media
    coverage of lynchings, 91, 93
    coverage of Trayvon Martin shooting, 128
    Japanese coverage of Korean crimes, 24
    Soviet Union, 111
Megale, Elizabeth, 132–134
Mexico
    Hughes' 1908 trip, 18, 80–81
    relocation of James Langston, 16, 18
"Midwinter Blues" (Hughes), 50–51

Miller, B.M., 69
  See also Scottsboro incident
Miller, R. Baxter, 16–27
Miller, W. Jason, 91–98
Minorities and voting laws, 117–125
Miscegenation. See Biracialism
"Misery" (Hughes), 60–61
Mississippi
  Till, Emmett, 95, 97, 98
  voting laws, 120
"Mississippi" (Hughes), 93, 98
Mississippi River, 45–46, 50
Modernism, 50
Montage of a Dream Deferred (Hughes), 25, 93
Montgomery, Olen, 69, 145
  See also Scottsboro incident
Moore, WilliAnn, 124
"Mother to Son" (Hughes), 41–42, 59–60
Mothers
  and biracial children in Hughes' works, 79–80
  "Mother to Son," 41–42, 59–60
  "The Negro Mother," 41–42, 66
"Mulatto" (Hughes), 21, 76–80
Mulattos. See Biracialism
Murray, Albert, 53
Music. See Blues music; Church music influence on Hughes; Jazz music

N

NAACP (National Association for the Advancement of Colored People)
  Hughes' work, 11
Ohio voting laws, 124
  Scottsboro incident, 101, 102
National poetry festivals, 96, 97
Native American heritage in Hughes' family, 18
Nature imagery in Hughes' work
  African motifs, 40
  "Dream Variations," 51
  "The Negro Speaks of Rivers," 45–46
  "Roland Hayes Beaten (Georgia: 1942)," 104
Nazi-Soviet Pact, 113
Nebraska voting laws, 119–120
"Negro." See "Proem" (Hughes)
"The Negro Artist and the Racial Mountain" (Hughes), 84, 108
"The Negro Mother" (Hughes), 41–42, 66
"The Negro Speaks of Rivers" (Hughes)
  American-ness, 50
  blues influence, 41
  dedication to Du Bois, 43, 46
  historical and cultural imagery, 45–46, 50, 85, 94–96
  lynching imagery, 94
  mysticism, 85–86
  publication in *Crisis*, 56
  voice element, 59
Nevada voting laws, 120
New Masses (magazine), 106
New Mexico voting laws, 120
"New Nationalism" (Roosevelt speech), 32
"New Negro," 10
  See also Harlem Renaissance
A New Song (collection; Hughes), 24–25, 48
"A New Song" (poem; Hughes), 66–67

Index

Nigerian literature, 98
Norden, Lawrence, 117–125
Norris, Clarence, 69
    pardon, 143, 144
    poem dedication, 11
    See also Scottsboro incident
North Carolina voting laws, 120, 124
"Not for Publication" (Hughes), 98

O

Obama, Barack, 138–139
Occupy movement, 135, 141
Ohio voting laws, 123–124
Oklahoma
    Hughes' family, 17
    self-defense laws, 133
O'Mara, Mark, 129
One-Way Ticket (collection; Hughes), 93–94
"One-Way Ticket" (poem; Hughes), 97
Onomatopoeia in "The Weary Blues," 19
"Open Letter to the South" (Hughes), 10
Oral traditions in Hughes' works, 55–62
    See also Folklore
Osawatomie, KS, 18, 31–32
L'Ouverture, Toussaint, 136–137

P

Pan-Africanism, 26
The Panther & the Lash (Hughes), 26–27
Pardoning of Scottsboro accused, 143–146
Parental rejection of biracial children, 21, 73–81
Paris trip, 26
Patronage, criticism of white, 106–108
Patterson, Haywood, 69, 144–145
    See also Scottsboro incident
Pennsylvania voting laws, 119
Perdomo, Willie, 52–53
"Personal" (Hughes), 65
Philanthropy, criticism of white, 106–108
Photo ID. *See* Identification, voter
Phylon (magazine), 86
Places in the Heart, 142
Poetics, 58–62
Poetry festivals, 96, 97
Police and implicit bias, 126, 132
Politics
    FBI security index, 26
    Glover, Danny, 135–142
    lynching poems and censorship, 91–98
    radical writings, 24, 99–114
    voting laws designed to diminished minority voters, 117–125
    See also Communism
Poverty
    Hughes' childhood, 16, 17–18, 33
    prostitution, 111
    voting laws, 117, 118–120
Powell, Ozie, 69, 145
    See also Scottsboro incident
"Prayer Meeting" (Hughes), 9, 66
Predator 2, 139
Prisoner rights, 141
"Proem" (Hughes), 40, 84, 92–93, 97

Prostitution, 24, 110–111
  See also Scottsboro incident
Protests. *See* Politics

R

Racial profiling. *See* Implicit bias; Racism
Racism
  black colleges, 22, 105
  defining discrimination, 129–130
  Hughes' black poetics and artistic process, 55–62
  Hughes' reaction to Southern, 10–11, 16, 22, 71, 88–89, 100
  implicit bias in Trayvon Martin shooting, 126–134
  lynching poems and censorship, 91–98
  radical writings by Hughes, 99–114
  rejection of biracial children in Hughes' works, 21, 73–81
  social messages in Hughes' poetry, 38–48
  tension between style and theme in Hughes' works, 82–90
  voting laws designed to diminished minority voters, 117–125
  See also Biracialism; Lynching poems; Scottsboro incident; Segregation
Radcliffe, Lucas, 22
Radical politics. *See* Communism
Radical writings of Langston Hughes, 99–114
"The Raid" (Hughes), 9
Rampersad, Arnold
  collection of Hughes' poetry, 9
  Communism, 101, 112, 114
  first blues music experience, 50
  Hughes' abolitionist ancestors and boyhood segregation, 28–36
Rape
  "Silhouette," 94, 97
  Washington, Jesse, 97
  See also Scottsboro incident
Rawls, Phillip, 143–146
Red baiting. *See* Anti-communism
Red scare. *See* Anti-communism
Reed, James W., 34
Reed, Mary "Auntie," 18, 34
Registration, voter, 117, 118, 122
Rejection of biracial children, 21, 73–81
Religion
  African American literature, 65–66
  church music, 9, 28, 35
  Hughes' criticism, 99, 109–110
  Hughes' involvement, 9, 34, 65
  Langston, Mary, 32
  Reed, Mary, 34
  segregation, 32, 64, 66–68
  spirituals, 9, 42, 51, 55, 60, 61, 65
  subject in Hughes' works, 64–72
  voting laws, 117, 123–125
  See also Christ imagery
Revolution, Haitian (1791–1804), 136–137
Revolution imagery
  anti-capitalist, 48, 109–110
  "Dream Variations," 52
  "Goodbye Christ," 109–110

"Roland Hayes Beaten (Georgia: 1942)," 104
"Tired," 109
Rhyme, 19, 60–61
Rhythm in African American culture
    Hughes' works, 55, 57, 61, 65, 66, 70, 85, 89
    Perdomo, 53
River imagery
    "The Bitter River," 46–47
    "The Negro Speaks of Rivers," 45–46, 50, 55, 86, 94–95
Roberson, Willie, 69, 145
    See also Scottsboro incident
Robeson, Paul, 137
Robinson, John, 145–146
Roessel, David, 9
"Roland Hayes Beaten (Georgia: 1942)" (Hughes), 103–104
Roosevelt, Theodore, 18, 32
Rosenwald Fund, 21
Roumain, Jacques, 56, 62
Russia. See Soviet Union trip

S

San Francisco State University, 137
Sandburg, Carl, 50
Saturday Review of Literature, 21
Scott, Rick, 128
Scottsboro Boys Museum and Cultural Center, 144, 145
"Scottsboro" (Hughes), 47–48
Scottsboro incident
    Communist Party, 101, 103
    lynching attempt, 145
    pardons for accused, 143–146
    photo of accused, 69
    silence of black colleges, 22
    as subject in Hughes' work, 10–11, 22, 47–48, 70–71, 101–103
Scottsboro Limited (Hughes), 11, 47, 48
Segregation
    Hughes' experiences, 28, 30–33, 35–36, 71, 88–89, 100
    patronage and philanthropy, 107–108
    religion, 32, 64, 66–68
    See also Lynching poems; Racism
Selected Poems (Hughes), 96, 97, 98
Self-defense laws and implicit bias, 126, 128, 132–134
Semple, Jesse B. See Simple, Jesse B. (Hughes character)
Senate Permanent Subcommittee on Investigations (1953), 11, 25, 91, 93–94, *107,* 112–114
Senghor, Léopold, 82–83
Sex, Race, and Class—The Perspective of Winning (James), 139
Sexuality, 29
Shakespeare in Harlem (Hughes), 25
Shanghai visit, 24
Shooter bias. See Implicit bias
"Silhouette" (Hughes), 94, 97
Simple, Jesse B. (Hughes character), 25–26, 61
Simple Takes a Wife (Hughes), 25
"Sinner" (Hughes), 66
Slavery
    abolitionists and Hughes' ancestors, 9, 28, 29, 31–32, *33*
    Haitian Revolution (1791-1804), 136–137

imagery, 66
religion, 64
See also Revolution imagery
Smith, Bessie, 52
Smith, Raymond, 82–90
Snipes, Wesley, 137
Social cognitions and bias, 130
Social messages in Hughes' poetry, 38–48
Socialism. See Communism
"Song for a Dark Girl" (Hughes), 71–72, 97
The Souls of Black Folk (Du Bois), 58, 84
The South
    Hughes' reaction to racism, 10–11, 16, 22, 71, 88–89, 100
    speaking tour, 21–22, 71, 83, 88–89, 102
    See also Great Migration; Lynching poems
"The South" (Hughes), 88–89, 97
South Africa and Haiti, 138
"Southern Gentlemen, White Prostitutes, Mill-Owners, and Negroes" (Hughes), 101–102
Soviet Union trip, 11, 16, 23–24, 110–112
    See also Communism
Spirituals
    "Feet o' Jesus," 60
    freedom imagery, 51
    influence on Hughes, 9, 42, 51, 55, 60, 61, 65
    "Mother to Son," 42
    "The Negro Mother," 42
Sports and segregation, 28, 32
Stairs imagery, 41–42, 59–60
"Stand your ground" laws and implicit bias, 126, 128, 132–134

Stereotypes
    African American literature, 38
    biracial, 74–77
    clown, 40
    implicit bias in shootings, 132
    meekness, 104
"Still Here" (Hughes), 96
Style and theme tension in Hughes' works, 82–90
Sudan protests, 141
Suicide, 81
Sullivan, Noel, 23, 24
"Summer Night" (Hughes), 40
Sunday voting restrictions, 117, 123–125
Syncopation, 50

T

Tension
    blues influence on Hughes, 50, 51
    between style and theme in Hughes' works, 82–90
Texas voting laws, 120–121, 123
Theme and style tension in Hughes' works, 82–90
"Three Lynching Songs" (Hughes), 98
Till, Emmett, 95, 97, 98
Time imagery in *The Weary Blues*, 84–85
"Tired" (Hughes), 109
"To Certain Negro Leaders" (Hughes), 106
Tokyo visit, 24
Toomer, Jean, 49
Topeka, KS, Hughes' childhood in, 18–19, 28, 30–31

Index

Translations by Hughes, 62
Treason accusations, 91
Turner, Nat, 47
2012 (film), 139

U

Understanding the New Black Poetry (Henderson), 51
United Nations Children's Fund (UNICEF), 135, 141
United States
    Haiti relations, 138
    Hughes' criticisms, 39–40
    imagery in "I, Too," 42–45
    voting laws are designed to diminished minority voters, 117–125
United Steelworkers, 140
Universities and colleges
    enrollment at Lincoln University, 21
    Glover, Danny protest, 137
    Hughes' criticisms, 22, 105–106
    positions, 25
    speaking tour, 21–22, 71, 83, 88–89, 102
University of Chicago, 25
University of North Carolina, 22, 71
Urbanization. *See* Great Migration
U.S. Congress, Hughes' ancestors, 28, 29
U.S. Defense Bonds, 25
U.S. Senate Permanent Subcommittee on Investigations (1953), 11, 25, 91, 93–94, *107,* 112–114
U.S. Supreme Court
    disparate treatment theory, 130

Marshall, Thurgood, 139
Scottsboro incident, 144
USSR. *See* Soviet Union trip

V

Video games and implicit bias studies, 131–132
Voting laws, and minority voters, 117–125
Voting Rights Act (1965), 121–122

W

Walker, Alice, 17
Walker, Margaret, 17
Wallace, George C., 144
Washington, Booker T., 31
Washington D.C. poetry festival (1962), 96, 97
Washington, Jesse, 97
Washington, Sheila, 145, 146
Wayne State University, 68
The Ways of White Folks (Hughes), 24
The Weary Blues (collection; Hughes)
    African American literary traditions, 56
    "As I Grew Older," 86
    "Cross," 21, 73, 75–76
    dual consciousness in, 84–85
    "Epilogue" ("I, Too"), 41, 42–45, 84
    glamorization of working-class, 106
    "Proem," 40, 84, 92–93, 97
    time imagery, 84–85
    "Youth," 84
"The Weary Blues" (poem; Hughes), 19–20, 35, 49, 84–85

Weems, Charlie, 69, 145
    See also Scottsboro incident
Weiser, Wendy R., 117–125
West Virginia. See Harpers Ferry raid (1859)
Where a Nickel Costs a Dime (Perdomo), 52–53
Whitman, Walt, 44–45, 50, 84, 85
Wilberforce, William, 136
Williams, Eugene, 69, 145
    See also Scottsboro incident
Williams, Sherley Anne, 52
Wisconsin voting laws, 119
Women
    biracial children in Hughes' works, 79–80
    "Mother to Son," 41–62, 59–60
    "The Negro Mother," 41–42, 66
    rights and Danny Glover, 135, 139
Soviet Union, 24, 110–111
Wright, Andy, 69, 102, 144–145
    See also Scottsboro incident
Wright, Richard, 39
Wright, Roy, 69, 144–145
    See also Scottsboro incident

Y

YMCA
    segregation, 28, 32
    speaking ban in Los Angeles, 68
"Youth" (Hughes), 85

Z

Zimmerman, George, 126–134

www.ingramcontent.com/pod-product-compliance
Lightning Source LLC
Chambersburg PA
CBHW071927290426
44110CB00013B/1502